Active Listening

R. R. Jordan

Collins ELT: London and Glasgow

Collins ELT
8 Grafton Street
London W1X 3LA

First published 1984
Last reprinted 1988

10 9 8 7 6 5 4 3

Phototypeset by Tradespools Ltd, Frome, Somerset
Printed in Great Britain by Hollen Street Press,
Slough, Berkshire

ISBN 0 00 370340 1

This book is accompanied by two cassettes
(ISBN 0 00 370341 X)

Design by Jacky Wedgwood
Cover design by Gina Smart
Illustrations by Gina Smart and Susan Neale

Contents

For Mother

By the same author

A Handbook for English Language Assistants
(with R. Mackay, Collins 1976)

Listening Comprehension and Note-Taking Course
(with K. James and A. J. Matthews, Collins 1979)

Reading in a Second Language
(with R. Mackay and B. Barkman, Newbury House 1979)

Looking for Information (Longman 1980)

Academic Writing Course (Collins 1980)

Figures in Language: Describe and Draw (Collins 1982)

Case Studies in ELT (editor, Collins 1983)

Acknowledgements

I am grateful to Teresa O'Brien and Terry McMylor for their assistance in recording material to go with the pilot version of this book. I am also grateful to Teresa O'Brien and Paul Barry for trying out some of the exercises with their students and for their constructive comments. In addition, I am grateful to Anthony Forrester, The English Centre, Eastbourne, for a critical reading of the manuscript, and to Gerry Abbott for some helpful suggestions. My grateful! thanks also go to some of my overseas students at the University of Manchester, in particular to Ximena Vidales Frias for kindly providing feedback on all the exercises.

I wish to express my gratitude to Marilyn Oates and Pat Abdallah for kindly typing the manuscript.

I am grateful to the British Council, London, for permission to make use of data from their publication *Statistics of Overseas Students in the UK, 1980/81* in Part 6, Exercise 1.

I found the following two books helpful in providing guidance for some of the exercises in Part 2: *Living English Speech* by W. Stannard Allen (Longman), and *Learning Rhythm and Stress* by M. Heliel and T. McArthur (Collins). In addition, I would recommend the following books to those who might wish for more detailed information and examples of English pronunciation: *Better English Pronunciation* by J. D. O'Connor (CUP), and *English Pronunciation* by Peter MacCarthy (Heffer/Cambridge) (out of print).

The publishers are grateful to the following for permission to reproduce photographs and other realia: The Ford Motor Company, photograph on page 50; Stanley Gibbons Limited, Penny Black on page 55; Keystone Press Agency Limited, photograph on page 34; the National Portrait Gallery, photograph on page 52; National Westminster Bank plc, cheques on page 37; the Post Office, photograph on page 56; the Savoy Hotel, photograph on page 35.

Using the book

Purpose

The main aim of the book and cassettes is to provide graded listening practice material to help students to improve their ability at understanding spoken English. It is hoped that students will increase their awareness of different features of the spoken language and become more sensitive to changes in sounds, stress, and intonation. In order to focus attention on certain aspects of the language, some writing activities are integrated with the listening. As the title of the book suggests, students will be 'doing something' while they are listening.

The spoken language is graded as follows: it is presented initially in individual sounds, then words and sentences and, finally, longer stretches of speech. The exercises are also graded: at first the emphasis is on *recognition* of sounds, stress and intonation; then some practice is given in *recognition together with writing or noting*. The material may be used, exercise by exercise, to supplement existing courses over a period of several weeks or months, or it may be used intensively on short courses. It may also be used for revision purposes.

In an introductory book of this size it has been necessary to be selective in the areas of spoken language chosen for practice. However, it is hoped that most of the areas that cause difficulty have been included. There is particular emphasis on: difficult individual sounds, especially when contrasted in pairs; contractions; weak forms in stress patterns; rising and falling intonation; and noting information given in short dialogues.

Learners

The learners will probably be teenagers or adults whose level of spoken English is elementary to intermediate. They may use English as a foreign or second language and may be studying in any part of the world. They may use the practice material individually, perhaps at home, or with a teacher in a class, or possibly in a language laboratory.

Organisation of the material

The cassettes
It is essential to have the two cassettes before the book can be used. The recorded material can be divided into two main sections: the first consists of Parts 1–3, and the second consists of Parts 4–6. In Parts 1 and 2 ('Sounds' and 'Stress and Intonation'), the speech is carefully produced, giving the learner time to listen carefully, and to get used to the voices. In Part 3 ('Practical Dialogues'), the spoken language is used more naturally in a number of different situations. In Parts 4–6 longer pieces of spoken language are used for descriptions, short talks, dialogues and interviews, together with a greater variety of exercises.

Although the main purpose of the cassettes is to provide listening material for exercises in the workbook, it is possible for students to use the cassettes as listening models for their own spoken English. This would be possible, particularly for Parts 1–3, and can be done by copying the cassettes into a language laboratory where the students can listen *and* repeat. They can, of course, listen and repeat with a personal cassette recorder, but their own voice will not be recorded.

Tape time
Tape 1   Side 1: Part 1–24 minutes
           Side 2: Part 2–21 minutes
Tape 2   Side 1: Part 3–34 minutes
           Side 2: Part 4–12 minutes
                      Part 5–7 minutes
                      Part 6–13 minutes

The workbook
Throughout the book there is a variety of exercises. The type of exercise changes according to the purpose of the Part. However, the main emphasis is upon listening, and therefore correct recognition of spoken language features. Thus, many of the early exercises require only a tick (√) to be used or a word underlined while later exercises need words or numbers to be written in spaces, or complete sentences to be written or notes to be taken. In addition, the later exercises are more complex and varied, sometimes requiring drawing or labelling.

The Answer Key is at the back of the book. It includes answers to all the exercises, together with some notes on particular difficulties. Students are recommended to check their answers carefully at the end of each exercise before going on to the next one. They should pay attention to details in the answers, such as correct spelling. The Answer Key also includes the transcript of all the dialogues, interviews etc. that are on the cassettes.

It is recommended that a good English dictionary is available for use in case some of the vocabulary is unknown. An English to mother-tongue dictionary will clearly be useful, but it will also be an advantage to have an English–English dictionary.

Part 1 Sounds

All the sounds of English are exemplified, in words, in contrasted words, and in sentences. Practice is given to particular difficulties e.g. final 's', final '-ed', and contractions e.g. 'doesn't'. Some use is made of phonetic symbols: they are helpful in drawing attention to the differences in sounds, but it is not necessary to write them. The Part ends with a grammatical summary of singular and plural forms: these are included because they commonly cause difficulty, both in speech and in writing.

Part 2 Stress and intonation

The main purpose of this Part is to help the learner to hear the differences between stress patterns, in words and in sentences, and thus to become more aware of, or sensitive to, changes in stress. This is done by selecting differences that are easier to hear and which are, in some cases, emphatic stress patterns. The normal stress patterns, with all their variations, are then used more naturally in the dialogues in Part 3. The examples of intonation patterns and the exercises on intonation provide an introduction to a rather complex subject. Again, in Part 3, intonation patterns are used naturally in the dialogues.

Part 3 Practical dialogues

Students frequently have difficulty in naming the letters of the English alphabet. Consequently, at the beginning of this Part there are some exercises on saying the names of the letters, for example, in the use of abbreviations. This is then linked to spelling people's names which are used in some of the dialogues. After this follows a variety of dialogue exercises, some of which include the use of numbers – another problem area for many students. At the end of the Part there are two longer dialogues which involve writing on a form.

In the dialogues it is important to notice the polite conventions that are used in the spoken language, for example, the appropriate use of 'please' and 'thank you'. If they are not used appropriately, it can immediately create an unfavourable impression with the listener. He may think that the speaker is being rude when, in fact, he does not intend to be. It is just as important, for the same reason, to try to use the correct stress and intonation patterns.

Part 4   Describe and draw or label

In this Part there are longer pieces of description and dialogue to listen to, and a variety of tasks to do: generally, they involve some kind of drawing or labelling. If parts of the exercises are found to be more difficult than others, the 'pause' or 'stop' button can be used on the cassette recorder to give more time to think or write. In addition, or instead of this, the passage may be listened to two or three times.

Part 5   Comparing information

The main purpose of the exercise is to develop the listener's ability to hear differences between sounds or words when they occur in longer pieces of spoken English compared with a written text. Full instructions are given for the exercises. Variations are possible, depending on the listener's language ability and memory: for example, for a more advanced use involving the use of memory, the passages can be listened to once and then read (instead of reading them at the same time as listening); and the actual changes in words can be written down instead of simply underlining the changed words.

Part 6   Information transfer

The exercises in this Part concentrate on listening carefully to longer talks and interviews, extracting certain pieces of information, and writing them in diagrams and tables. Some of the information that has to be written is numbers, sometimes in the form of times and dates. This is to give practice to the many students who have difficulty in writing numbers when listening to them.

Finally . . . Remember that the difficulty level of the exercises can be adjusted to the language level of the learner in several ways, for example:

1   the tapes can be listened to one, two or three times before writing an exercise;
2   the tape can be stopped to give time to write, or the writing can be done while the tape is playing;
3   an additional use of the scripted dialogues in the Answer Key is that they can be *read at the same time as listening* to the cassette (after the exercises have been completed). This can help the student in a number of ways, particularly in showing how the words are grouped for speech with the breath pauses, and thus helping him/her to improve fluency. It can also help to improve the silent reading speed.

Part 1 Sounds

Introduction

In this part you will be asked to listen to the *sounds* of English. The exercises will check your recognition and understanding of what you hear. In some of the exercises you will be asked to put a *tick* (√) or a *cross* (X) or to underline; in others you will be asked to write some words or sentences. Listen to your cassette when you see 'Listen' in the left-hand margin.

1 The sounds of English

There are usually 44 *sounds* in English. They are divided into groups of sounds. Look at the list of words below. One sound is underlined in each word (and the phonetic symbol for that sound is given after the word). Now listen.

Listen

Group 1

1	pen	/p/	9	fall	/f/	17	hot	/h/
2	bad	/b/	10	very	/v/	18	my	/m/
3	ten	/t/	11	thin	/θ/	19	no	/n/
4	day	/d/	12	they	/ð/	20	sing	/ŋ/
5	key	/k/	13	so	/s/	21	let	/l/
6	get	/g/	14	zoo	/z/	22	red	/r/
7	cheap	/tʃ/	15	she	/ʃ/	23	yes	/j/
8	jump	/dʒ/	16	pleasure	/ʒ/	24	wet	/w/

Exercise 1

You will hear 10 pairs of words containing some of the above sounds. If the two words in each pair are the *same*, put a *tick* √ in the box. If the words are *different*, put a *cross* X.

Example: if you heard these words – safe/save – put X

– safe/safe – put √

Listen

1 ☐   3 ☐   5 ☐   7 ☐   9 ☐

2 ☐   4 ☐   6 ☐   8 ☐   10 ☐

Look at the lists of words below.

Listen

Group 2

1	see	/iː/	3	bed	/e/	5	arm	/ɑː/
2	it	/ɪ/	4	man	/æ/	6	got	/ɒ/

7	s<u>aw</u>	/ɔː/	9	s<u>oo</u>n	/uː/	11	l<u>ear</u>n	/ɜː/
8	p<u>u</u>t	/ʊ/	10	c<u>u</u>p	/ʌ/	12	<u>a</u>bout	/ə/

Group 3

1	p<u>a</u>ge	/eɪ/	4	n<u>ow</u>	/aʊ/	7	th<u>ere</u>	/eə/
2	h<u>o</u>me	/əʊ/	5	b<u>oy</u>	/ɔɪ/	8	t<u>our</u>	/ʊə/
3	f<u>i</u>ve	/aɪ/	6	h<u>ere</u>	/ɪə/			

Exercise 2

You will hear 10 pairs of words containing some of the above sounds. If the two words in each pair are the *same*, put a *tick* ☑ in the space. If the words are *different*, put a *cross* ☒.

Listen

1 ☐ 3 ☐ 5 ☐ 7 ☐ 9 ☐

2 ☐ 4 ☐ 6 ☐ 8 ☐ 10 ☐

2 Some pairs of sounds

Exercise 3

Look at the pairs of words below. Only one sound is different in each pair. (Phonetic symbols of the sounds that are different are given in brackets after the words.)

After each pair of words one of the words is said again. When you hear that word <u>underline</u> the correct word. The first one is done as an example.

Listen

Example: <u>pie</u>/buy (p/b)

1	put/foot	(p/f)	11	cheap/jeep	(tʃ/dʒ)
2	boat/vote	(b/v)	12	leave/live	(iː/ɪ)
3	fan/van	(f/v)	13	bill/bell	(ɪ/e)
4	town/down	(t/d)	14	men/man	(e/æ)
5	tin/thin	(t/θ)	15	hat/heart	(æ/ɑː)
6	day/they	(d/ð)	16	pot/port	(ɒ/ɔː)
7	teeth/teethe	(θ/ð)	17	far/four	(ɑː/ɔː)
8	could/good	(k/g)	18	hot/hut	(ɒ/ʌ)
9	price/prize	(s/z)	19	cup/cap	(ʌ/æ)
10	see/she	(s/ʃ)	20	walk/work	(ɔː/ɜː)

Exercise 4

Only *one* word is said from each of the following pairs of words. <u>Underline</u> the word that you hear.

Listen

1	pat/bat	4	beat/bit	8	rich/ridge
2	ten/den	5	match/march	9	bed/bad
3	sue/zoo	6	few/view	10	lock/luck
		7	came/game		

Exercise 5

Read the following pairs of sentences. *One sentence* will be read out only once from each pair of sentences. Notice that there is only one word different in each pair (it is underlined). *Tick* $\boxed{\checkmark}$ the sentence that you hear.

Listen

1a She is <u>living</u> with her brother. ☐
 b She is <u>leaving</u> with her brother. ☐

2a His <u>cup</u> was very dirty. ☐
 b His <u>cap</u> was very dirty. ☐

3a Has the <u>boss</u> arrived yet? ☐
 b Has the <u>bus</u> arrived yet? ☐

4a He <u>hit</u> the ball in the garden. ☐
 b He <u>hid</u> the ball in the garden. ☐

5a What do you think of the <u>prices</u>? ☐
 b What do you think of the <u>prizes</u>? ☐

Revision: Dictation

Exercise 6

On your cassette you will hear some words. Each word is said only once. *Write* below the words that you hear. If necessary stop the cassette to give yourself time to write. Check your spelling carefully.

Listen

1 _____	8 _____	15 _____
2 _____	9 _____	16 _____
3 _____	10 _____	17 _____
4 _____	11 _____	18 _____
5 _____	12 _____	19 _____
6 _____	13 _____	20 _____
7 _____	14 _____	

3 Some sounds at the ends of words

i) The letters 's' or 'es' at the end of words can be pronounced in three ways: /s/, /z/, or /ɪz/. Look at the following examples.

Listen

a book<u>s</u> ⎫
   stop<u>s</u> ⎬ /s/
   Frank'<u>s</u> ⎭

b dog<u>s</u> ⎫
   see<u>s</u> ⎬ /z/
   Bob'<u>s</u> ⎭

c glass<u>es</u> ⎫
   lose<u>s</u> ⎬ /ɪz/
   George'<u>s</u> ⎭

Exercise 7

Listen

The following 10 words are in mixed order. After you have listened *write* the words in the correct groups below according to the way the letters 's' or 'es' are pronounced at the end of each word.

10 words	Group **a** – /s/	Group **b** – /z/	Group **c** – /ɪz/
lives			
watches			
beds			
eats			
says			
coughs			
kicks			
bridges			
boys			
dishes			

ii) The letters 'ed' at the end of words can be pronounced in three ways: /t/, /d/ or /ɪd/. Look at the following examples.

Listen

a looked
stopped } /t/
touched

b stored
showed } /d/
robbed

c started
added } /ɪd/

Exercise 8

Listen

The following 10 words are in mixed order. After you have listened *write* the words in the correct groups below according to the way the letters 'ed' are pronounced at the end of each word.

10 words	Group **a** – /t/	Group **b** – /d/	Group **c** – /ɪd/
wanted			
worked			
pushed			
closed			
kissed			
opened			
climbed			
demanded			
played			
hired			

4 Contractions

Look at the following list of 24 words (all are verb forms).

am	are	is	were	was	shall	will	
should	would	have	has	had			
do	does	did	can	could	may	might	
must	ought	need	dare	used			

Each of these words can be combined with another word. The combination is then pronounced as one word.

Example: I have → I've; do not → don't.

These are called *contractions*. Contractions can be *affirmative* or *negative*. They are very common in everyday spoken English.

Affirmatives
The following are examples of affirmative contractions:

Listen

am, are, is
1 I am → I'm
2 you are → you're
3 he is → he's
she is → she's
it is → it's
4 we are → we're
5 they are → they're

shall, will
6 I shall/will → I'll
7 he / she shall/will → he'll / she'll
8 we shall/will → we'll

have, has
9 I have → I've
10 he / she has → he's / she's
11 they have → they've

should, would, had
12 I should → I'd
13 he would → he'd
she had → she'd
14 you → you'd

Exercise 9

Look at the four pairs of sentences below. One sentence from each pair will be read – only once. *Tick* the sentence that you hear.

Listen

1a	You're here.	☐	**3a**	She'll go.	☐
b	You'll hear.	☐	**b**	She'd go	☐
2a	We're ready.	☐	**4a**	I've written.	☐
b	They're ready.	☐	**b**	I'd written.	☐

Negatives
The 24 verb forms listed above may be combined with the weak form /nt/ of 'not' to make negative contractions.

Listen

1	aren't	9	haven't	17	mayn't
2	isn't	10	hasn't	18	mightn't
3	weren't	11	hadn't	19	mustn't
4	wasn't	12	don't	20	oughtn't
5	shan't (= shall not)	13	doesn't	21	needn't
6	won't (= will not)	14	didn't	22	daren't
7	shouldn't	15	can't	23	usedn't
8	wouldn't	16	couldn't		

Note

1 'am' does not contract with 'not'.
The negative is 'I'm not', and the negative question is 'Aren't I?'
2 'mayn't' and 'usedn't' are not often heard now. 'May' is usually spoken in its full form: 'You may – you may not'. The negative of 'used' can also be 'didn't use'.

Exercise 10

Look at the four pairs of sentences below. One sentence from each pair will be read – only once. *Tick* the sentence that you hear.

Listen

1a They aren't going. ☐ 3a You haven't done it. ☐
 b They weren't going. ☐ b You hadn't done it. ☐

2a I shan't get it. ☐ 4a He couldn't do it. ☐
 b I can't get it. ☐ b He wouldn't do it. ☐

Exercise 11a

Look at the ten pairs of sentences below. One sentence from each pair will be read – only once. *Tick* the sentence that you hear.

Listen

1a He's sitting on the floor. ☐ 5a I'll buy it for you. ☐
 b She's sitting on the floor. ☐ b I'd buy it for you. ☐

2a She walked every day. ☐ 6a She isn't like her father. ☐
 b She's walked every day. ☐ b She doesn't like her father. ☐

3a He'll finish it later. ☐ 7a They don't want the books. ☐
 b We'll finish it later. ☐ b They won't want the books. ☐

4a He hadn't received the money. ☐ 8a It was a glass. ☐
 b He hasn't received the money. ☐ b It wasn't glass. ☐

14

9a	They can do it.	☐	**10a**	He isn't washing up.	☐
b	They can't do it.	☐	**b**	He wasn't washing up.	☐

Exercise 11b

The following three sentences are taken from Exercise 11a. Read them and choose the correct meaning for 's and 'd. *Tick* the correct box.

1 He's sitting on the floor. *means* He is ☐ *or* He has ☐

2 She's walked every day. *means* She is ☐ *or* She has ☐

3 I'd buy it for you. *means* I $\begin{cases} \text{should} \\ \text{would} \end{cases}$ ☐ *or* I had ☐

Exercise 12

Listen

You will hear five pairs of sentences. The two sentences in each pair will be read once. If the two sentences are the same, *tick* 'same'; if they are different, *tick* 'different'.

1a
b   same ☐   different ☐   **4a**
b   same ☐   different ☐

2a
b   same ☐   different ☐   **5a**
b   same ☐   different ☐

3a
b   same ☐   different ☐

5 Singular and plural: grammatical summary

Look at the following notes carefully:

i) *countable* nouns (which take a plural verb form for the plural):
Example: students, books, eggs, boys.

ii) *uncountable* nouns (which do *not* take a plural verb form):
Example: advice, news, information, butter, water.

iii) *other words:*
a *singular*: this, that
plural: these, those

b some
a lot of $\Big|$ + countable **or** uncountable nouns

c a few   + countable noun

d a little   + uncountable noun

e another   = *singular*
others   = *plural*
(the) other = *singular or plural*

In the following examples notice whether the words are used in the singular or plural. Notice also how verbs are used with these words.

Listen

There were only a few boys there.

1 This question is very difficult.

2 These are the answers to the questions.

3 That student likes singing.

4 Those students aren't studying.

5 He asked for some advice.

6 She bought some books.

7 The news isn't very good.

8 There are a lot of marks on the table.

9 There's a lot of noise in the room.

10 There was a little butter in the dish.

11 There wasn't any water in the glass.

12 There were only a few boys there.

13 He works in the other room.

14 She lives in another town.

15 The others live in the next street.

Dictation: singular and plural

Exercise 13

In this exercise you will hear eight sentences. As you hear the sentences write them below. Each is read only once. Stop the cassette after each sentence to give yourself time to write. Check your answers carefully.

Listen

1 _____

2 _____

3 _____

4 _____

5 _____

6 _____

7 _____

8 _____

Part 2 Stress and intonation

1 Short stress patterns

The rhythm of spoken English consists of *stressed* (strong) and *unstressed* (weak) words or parts of words (syllables). The strong and weak syllables and words combine to form patterns.

Syllables or words which have a *strong* stress are marked — and those which are *weak* are marked ●. The *strong* stress will often seem louder or longer; the *weak* stress will often seem quieter or shorter.

Look at the two groups of words below. Notice the different stress patterns.

Listen

Group **a**	*Group* **b**
— ●	● —
find it	they know
phone him	it's mine
tell me	we walked
show her	she's nice
write it	it rained

Exercise 1

You will hear the following words on your cassette. Above each word or syllable write the correct stress mark:
‾ for a *strong* stress, ● for a *weak* stress. If necessary stop the cassette to give yourself time to write.

Listen

Example: stop it
          — ●

1	tell her	5	a book	8	help him
2	the desk	6	we'll try	9	send it
3	it's old	7	his shoes	10	he's in
4	got it				

Exercise 2

Five pairs of words are said on the cassette similar to the examples at the beginning of Part 2. Write on the next page the pairs of words that you hear. Put them in the correct column according to the stress pattern shown **a** or **b**. If necessary stop the cassette to give yourself time to write.

Listen

a
— ●

b
● —

_____   _____
_____   _____
_____   _____

2   Longer stress patterns

Notice the different stress patterns in the following examples on your cassette.

Listen

    ● — ● ●
1 She's eaten it all.
2 He wanted her to.

    ● — ● ● —
3 He's read all the books.
4 I think that he's good.

    ● — ● — ●
5 It's time for dinner.
6 The plate is broken.

'What happened to Sarah's birthday cake?'
'She's eaten it all.'

'Do you think David will pass the exam?'
'He's read all the books.'

Note	The words in the examples above that have the *strong stress* supply most of the *information* in the sentence. Example: In no. 3 'read' and 'books' are the most important words. In no. 6 'plate' and 'broken' are the most important words.

Exercise 3

Read the following sentences carefully. <u>Underline</u> the words in each sentence that you think give most of the information.

1 We travelled by train.
2 A cup of coffee.
3 He'll give you another one.
4 She hasn't been before.
5 You're wanted on the phone.

These sentences are on your cassette. After you have listened to them, write above each word or syllable the *strong stress* mark ‾ where you hear a strong stress.

Listen

Compare the words you have marked with a strong stress with the words that you underlined from your reading.

3 Noun stress

a Nouns with two syllables usually have the *strong stress* on the *first syllable*. Look at the following examples.

Listen

1	teacher	5	mountain	9	matches	12	houses
2	doctor	6	student	10	pages	13	letters
3	lecture	7	language	11	places	14	neighbours
4	tutor	8	boxes				

b Nouns with three syllables also usually have the *strong stress* on the *first syllable*.

Listen

alphabet   minister   catalogue
photograph   industry

Exercise 4

Read the following list of 10 words and then write them in the correct group according to the *number of syllables* they have.

10 words	— ● (2 syllables)	— ● ● (3 syllables)
lecturer		
principal		
college		
English		
sentence		
paragraph		
essay		
travel		
holiday		
ticket		

Listen

Compare the answers to see if your groups are correct.

4 Variable stress

a The strong stress may be on other syllables (i.e. not always the first one).

Listen

a	b	c
● — ●	● —●●	● ●—●●
suggestion	majority	possibility
election	publicity	opportunity

> **Note**
>
> 1 In nouns ending in '-ion', as in group **a** above, the strong stress falls on the syllable *immediately before* the suffix '-ion'.
> 2 In nouns ending in '-ity', as in groups **b** and **c** above, the strong stress falls on the syllable *immediately before* the suffix '-ity'.

b When words of related meaning change their grammatical form e.g. noun to adjective, the stress pattern may change.

Listen

	a	b
	● — ● ●	● ● — ●
1	economy	economic
	● — ● ●	● ● — ●
2	economist	economics
	● — ● ●	● ● — ●●
3	economize	economical

> **Note**
>
> When the following suffixes are added to the end of nouns to form adjectives, the strong stress falls on the syllable *immediately before* them.
> '-ic', '-ical'
> '-cial', '-tial'
> '-cient', '-cious', '-tious'

Exercise 5

You will hear some more words on your cassette. Write in the *strong* and *weak* stress marks above the words in **b** below.

Listen

	a	b
	— ● ●	
4	industry	industrial
	— ● ●	
5	politics	political
	— ●● ●	
6	agriculture	agricultural

5 Verb stress

Verbs of two syllables. These may have the *strong stress* on the first *or* second syllable. The stress will be on the syllable which contains the *root* of the verb.

<table>
<tr><td>**Note**</td><td>The root may be a word itself
Example: 'hard' in 'har<u>den</u>'
or a root in other words
Example: '-ject' in 'pro<u>ject</u>' and 're<u>ject</u>'
or the other syllable is a common prefix or suffix
Example: '<u>pre</u>fer' and '<u>dis</u>miss'.</td></tr>
</table>

Pattern 1: strong stress on the *first* syllable.

Listen

— ●

1	cover	5	harden
2	bother	6	soften
3	finish	7	frighten
4	publish	8	happen

Pattern 2: strong stress on the *second* syllable.

Listen

● —

1	prepare	5	perform
2	propose	6	enjoy
3	belong	7	mislead
4	distrust	8	retire

Exercise 6

You will hear 10 verbs. Write them in the correct pattern column.

Listen

verbs	*Pattern 1* — ●	*Pattern 2* ● —
advise	_____	_____
promote	_____	_____
brighten	_____	_____
believe	_____	_____
punish	_____	_____
translate	_____	_____
receive	_____	_____
shorten	_____	_____
excuse	_____	_____
polish	_____	_____

<table>
<tr><td>**Note**</td><td>See the notes in the Key for more information and for patterns for verbs with more than two syllables.</td></tr>
</table>

6 Noun and verb stress

There are several words, mostly of two syllables, which have
1 the *main stress* at the *beginning* when they are *nouns* (or *adjectives*), and
2 the *main stress* at the *end* when they are *verbs*. The spelling is the same in both cases. Examples:

Listen

1 What is that *object*? (noun)

2 Do you *object* to the idea? (verb)

Exercise 7

Read carefully the following sentences. In each sentence there is a word in *italics*. Write the *main stress* mark above the correct syllable in the word, as in the examples you have just seen. Remember . . . you must decide if the word is a noun or a verb.

1 Terry will *record* your voice on tape.

2 Metals *contract* when the temperature falls.

3 These goods are for *export* only.

4 She's making good *progress* in English.

5 Prices continue to *increase* each year.

Exercise 8

Each word below will be said once only. Write the *main stress* mark above the syllable that contains the strong stress in each word.

Listen

1 protest	4 transport	7 survey	9 subject
2 present	5 object	8 produce	10 frequent
3 desert	6 accent		

7 Significant stress

Significant stress in a sentence is on the word that is the most important for the *speaker's meaning*. The stress may be on almost any word and may indicate the speaker's feelings, emotions or attitudes. Read the following examples carefully.

Listen

Significant stress <u>underlined</u>	Possible meaning
1 <u>I</u> don't live in London.	but <u>he</u> does
2 I <u>don't</u> live in London.	<u>yes</u>, you do!
3 I don't <u>live</u> in London.	but I <u>work</u> there
4 I don't live <u>in</u> London.	I live in the <u>suburbs</u>
5 I don't live in <u>London</u>.	I live in <u>Brighton</u>

Exercise 9

Listen

You will hear the same sentence four times. Each sentence has a different meaning. <u>Underline</u> the word in each sentence below that carries the significant stress.

1   Did Tony buy that black car?

2   Did Tony buy that black car?

3   Did Tony buy that black car?

4   Did Tony buy that black car?

Exercise 10a

Listen

You will hear some short dialogues on the telephone. The first speaker answers the phone, giving his/her number. The second speaker apologises for having dialled the wrong number, and then says the number that he/she wanted. A significant stress is put on the figure that was wrong.
Example: '485 4973'
         'Sorry, I wanted 485 49<u>6</u>3 (the wrong figure here is <u>6</u>)
Write in the space next to each telephone number the single figure that is wrong.

a	273 3095	_____	d	27634	_____
b	126 2812	_____	e	409 3417	_____
c	653 7285	_____	f	57981	_____

Exercise 10b

Listen

This is a similar exercise to 10a. However, this time you will hear only one person, who apologises for having dialled the wrong number. A significant stress is put on the wrong figure.
Example: 'Sorry, I wanted 297 <u>5</u>613'.
Write in the spaces below the single figure that was dialled wrongly.

a	_____	b	_____	c	_____
d	_____	e	_____	f	_____

8   Essential weak stress forms

i)   In fluent, connected speech many smaller words in English change their stress, from strong to *weak*. It is normally the vowel sound that changes. For example, the word 'some' often changes from its strong stress form /sʌm/ to the *weak stress form* /səm/. The most commonly used weak form is the vowel sound /ə/ as at the beginning of '<u>a</u>bout' or '<u>a</u>go', or at the end of 'bett<u>er</u>' or 'doll<u>ar</u>'.

Exercise 11

When you hear the sentences below, decide if the underlined word in each is spoken with a *weak stress* form (as in ordinary speech) or a *strong stress* form (for particular emphasis). *Tick* the appropriate box.

Listen

		strong stress	weak stress
1	He <u>was</u> late.	☐	☐
2	She <u>must</u> go.	☐	☐
3	Look at <u>her</u>.	☐	☐
4	Where <u>does</u> he live?	☐	☐
5	They <u>have</u> lost it.	☐	☐

ii) The words listed below are very commonly used in spoken English. In fluent speech they nearly always have a *weak stress* as shown here.

Listen

1 Articles
1 a   /ə/   <u>a</u> book
2 an   /ən/   <u>an</u> apple
3 the   /ðə/ *or* /ðɪ/   <u>the</u> teacher
    <u>the</u> animal
4 some   /səm/   <u>some</u> money

2 Pronouns
1 me   /mɪ/   help <u>me</u>
2 he   /hɪ/   <u>he</u> didn't
3 her   /(h)ə/   tell <u>her</u>
4 us   /(ə)s/   show <u>us</u>
5 them   /ðəm/   buy <u>them</u>

3 Conjunctions
1 and   /(ə)n(d)/   fish <u>and</u> chips
2 as   /əz/   hard <u>as</u> iron
3 but   /bət/   strict <u>but</u> fair
4 than   /ðən/   younger <u>than</u> him
5 that   /ðət/   so <u>that</u> she could

4 Prepositions
1 at   /ət/   look <u>at</u> him
2 for   /fə/   it's <u>for</u> you
3 from   /frəm/   it's <u>from</u> us
4 of   /əv/   out <u>of</u> here
5 to   /tə/   go <u>to</u> bed

5 Auxiliary verbs
1 am   /əm/   I <u>am</u> tired.
2 was   /wəz/   She <u>was</u> there.
3 were   /wə/   You <u>were</u> wrong.
4 shall   /ʃəl/   We <u>shall</u> win.
5 have   /(h)əv/   They <u>have</u> gone.
6 has   /(h)əz/   He <u>has</u> finished.

7 had   /(h)əd/   They <u>had</u> paid.
8 can   /kən/   I <u>can</u> go.
9 must   /məs(t)/   We <u>must</u> stop.
10 do   /də/ *or* /dʊ/   <u>Do</u> you like it?
11 does   /dəz/   What <u>does</u> he want?

Note
These are in addition to those verb forms listed in Part 1.4
Contractions.

Note	1	In general, *content words* usually have a strong stress (that is, nouns, adjectives, verbs and adverbs).
	2	*Structural words* are usually unstressed (that is, articles, pronouns, conjunctions, prepositions, and auxiliary verbs).
	3	You will notice the weak forms above being used in *Part 3 Practical dialogues*.

Exercise 12

Listen

In the spaces in the following sentences write in the *weak forms* (in full) that you hear on the cassette. Each blank indicates one word.

1   She says ＿＿＿ ＿＿＿ ＿＿＿ got one.

2   ＿＿＿ dog ran out ＿＿＿ ＿＿＿ house.

3   He ＿＿＿ older ＿＿＿ ＿＿＿ others.

4   There ＿＿＿ ＿＿＿ lot ＿＿＿ ＿＿＿ other school.

5   Give it ＿＿＿ ＿＿＿ ＿＿＿ soon ＿＿＿ possible.

Revision: dictation

Exercise 13

Write below the eight sentences that you hear on your cassette. They will contain some of the weak forms that you have just listened to. Write the words that you hear in their *full form* (not contracted form). Stop the cassette after each sentence to give yourself time to write. After you have finished writing, listen again to the sentences and <u>underline</u> all the essential weak stress forms that you hear.

Listen

1   ＿＿＿＿＿＿＿＿＿＿＿＿＿＿＿＿＿＿＿＿＿＿＿＿

2   ＿＿＿＿＿＿＿＿＿＿＿＿＿＿＿＿＿＿＿＿＿＿＿＿

3   ＿＿＿＿＿＿＿＿＿＿＿＿＿＿＿＿＿＿＿＿＿＿＿＿

4   ＿＿＿＿＿＿＿＿＿＿＿＿＿＿＿＿＿＿＿＿＿＿＿＿

5   ＿＿＿＿＿＿＿＿＿＿＿＿＿＿＿＿＿＿＿＿＿＿＿＿

6   ＿＿＿＿＿＿＿＿＿＿＿   ＿＿＿＿＿＿＿＿＿＿＿＿

7   ＿＿＿＿＿＿＿＿＿＿＿＿＿＿＿＿＿＿＿＿＿＿＿＿

8   ＿＿＿＿＿＿＿＿＿＿＿＿＿＿＿＿＿＿＿＿＿＿＿＿

Check your answers carefully.

9 Intonation patterns

Intonation is the changing pitch, or rising and falling, of the voice. English intonation patterns are of two main types. Both types usually begin fairly high and then fall until the last *significant* stress. Type 1 then *falls* at the end; Type 2 *rises* at the end.

a You will now hear some one-word examples of Type 1. This mark: (ˋ) indicates falling intonation.

Listen

ˋNo.   ˋStop.   ˋWhere?   ˋWhy?   ˋGood.

b Now listen to some examples of Type 2. This mark: (ˌ) indicates rising intonation.

Listen

ˌMe?   ˌThese?   ˌTwo?   ˌHis?   ˌWho?

Exercise 14

In this exercise some words are spoken with a falling intonation and some with a rising one. Put a mark in the box in front of each word to show if it is *falling* [\\] or *rising* [/].

Listen

☐him?   ☐yes   ☐mine   ☐whose?   ☐wait   ☐right

Type 1: falling intonation (ˋ)
This pattern is often used for *questions beginning with a question-word* (e.g. 'Where?'), *orders*, and *definite remarks*. Look at the following questions and responses.

Listen

1 What's the ˋtime? I don't ˋknow.

2 Where has she ˋgone? To visit her ˋaunt.

3 Which is ˋyours? The one on the ˋshelf.

4 Who's the ˋauthor? A man called ˋBrown.

Type 2: rising intonation (ˌ)
This pattern is often used for *questions* that can be answered 'yes' or 'no' (those *beginning with an auxiliary verb*). It is also used for *statements* made as *requests*, for apologies, and some other emotions.

Listen

1 Do you ˌknow?   6 That's ˌright.

2 Are you ˌready?   7 Good ˌbye.

3 Can I ˌhelp you?   8 I beg your ˌpardon?

4 Does she ˌlike it?   9 Please sit ˌdown.

5 Will you be ˌfree tomorrow?   10 If you ˌlike.

Exercise 15

Some of the following sentences are spoken with a falling intonation and some with a rising intonation. Mark the main fall (ˋ) or rise (ˏ) in the correct place in each sentence.

Listen

1 Why are you so late?

2 Must you go now?

3 Are you happy?

4 He'll be along later.

5 Do you mind if I smoke?

6 How far is it to London?

10 Intonation and meaning

It is important to have the correct intonation. If the wrong intonation pattern is used it may change the meaning. Examples:

Listen

1a ˏSorry? (a question, perhaps asking for repetition)

 b ˋSorry. (an apology)

2a ˏPardon? (a question, as above)

 b (I beg your) ˋpardon. (an apology)·

Exercise 16

Each of the words below will be said once, either with a *rising* or a *falling intonation*. Decide on the general meaning of what you hear and *tick* the appropriate box for a *question/exclamation* or a *statement/answer*.

Listen

	question/exclamation	statement/answer
1 Yes	☐	☐
2 Here	☐	☐
3 These	☐	☐
4 Five	☐	☐
5 Me	☐	☐

Part 3 Practical dialogues

Introduction

In this part you will be given some practice in writing names of people and places, times, dates, (telephone) numbers, and prices. Names of people and places are never easy to spell. Try your best, and where necessary guess. Many of the exercises are in the form of short dialogues.

1 The letters of the alphabet

The English alphabet has 26 *letters*. On your cassette you will hear how to say them.

Listen

CAPITAL LETTERS: A B C D E F G H I J K L M N O P Q R S T U V W X Y Z

small letters: a b c d e f g h i j k l m n o p q r s t u v w x y z

Exercise 1

In this exercise 10 letters are said once each, in a mixed order. Write them in the spaces below in CAPITAL LETTERS.

Listen

| 1 _____ | 3 _____ | 5 _____ | 7 _____ | 9 _____ |
| 2 _____ | 4 _____ | 6 _____ | 8 _____ | 10 _____ |

2 Some common abbreviations

Some common abbreviations are given below. On your cassette you will hear how to say them.

Listen

| 1 BBC | 3 GB | 5 SOS | 7 UN | 9 USSR |
| 2 EEC | 4 ILO | 6 UK | 8 USA | 10 WHO |

Exercise 2

On your cassette someone is asking what the letters in 10 abbreviations represent or mean in the question 'What does . . . stand for?' After each question write only the *abbreviation* that you hear in the space below (not the question or meaning).

Listen

| 1 _____ | 3 _____ | 5 _____ | 7 _____ | 9 _____ |
| 2 _____ | 4 _____ | 6 _____ | 8 _____ | 10 _____ |

3 Form-filling: personal information

On your cassette you will hear a secretary speaking to a student. She is asking him for information in order to complete an application form for a course. First, listen to the dialogue.

Listen

When you have finished, rewind your cassette to the beginning of the dialogue. As you listen again, look at the Application Form below. Notice which information has been included and where it has been written.

Listen

```
Surname   SVENSSON
(in CAPITAL LETTERS)

First name   Arvid

Male/female (underline as appropriate)

Country   Sweden

Mother tongue   Swedish

Age   40
```

Part of an application form.

Exercise 3

On your cassette you will hear another dialogue which is similar to the first one. At the same time as you are listening try to write the appropriate information on the form below.

Listen

```
Surname _____
(in CAPITAL LETTERS)

First name _____

Male/female (underline as appropriate)

Country _____

Mother tongue _____

Age _____
```

4 Time

Listen

a Excuse me. Can you tell me the time, please?
Yes, it's eight o'clock.

b What time do the banks close today, please?
Half past three.

Note	In the following exercise the words *past* and *to* are used as in the diagram to indicate minutes *past* or *to* the hour. 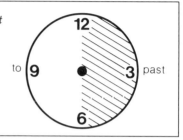

Exercise 4

In the short dialogues that follow you will hear someone ask a question about the time. When the answer is given *draw the time* on the clock faces below.
Example: Excuse me. What's the time, please?
It's a quarter past six.

Listen

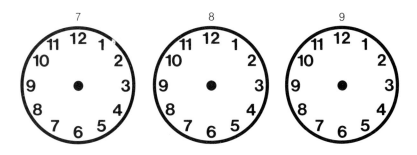

5 Time and travel

For travel by train, plane or ship, the time is usually given by the 24-hour clock.

Example: 1.30 p.m. is 13.30
               3.45 p.m. is 15.45
               7.15 p.m. is 19.15
              11.55 p.m. is 23.55

Listen

a When does the London train arrive, please?
    Ten thirty-five.   (10.35)

b Do you know what time the next flight is to Manchester?
    I think it's thirteen-thirty.   (13.30)

Exercise 5

There are some questions and answers about time on your cassette. When you hear the answers *tick* the appropriate times in the boxes below.

Listen

1	11.13	
	11.30	

2	12.15	
	12.50	

3	14.14	
	14.40	

4	22.15	
	22.50	

5	17.13	
	17.30	

Exercise 6

On your cassette you will hear some announcements from railway stations and airports. These announcements give information to travellers about trains and planes. For each announcement that you hear write in the box below the platform/flight number, time and destination. Stop the cassette to give yourself time to write. (The first one has been done as an example.)

Trains

	Platform number	Time	Destination
1	2	15.40	*Birmingham*
2			
3			
4			
5			

Planes

	Flight number	Time	Destination
6			
7			
8			
9			
10			

6 Dates

a The *days of the week* are as follows. On your cassette you will hear how to say them.

Sunday Monday Tuesday Wednesday Thursday Friday Saturday

b The *months of the year* are as follows:

January February March April May June July August September October November December

c The numbers 1, 2, 3, at the end of dates are usually written 1st (first), 2nd (second), 3rd (third) – also in 21st, 31st, 22nd, 23rd. The other dates are written with 'th' after them – 4th, 12th, 20th, etc.

d Look at the following dialogues:

1 When are you leaving?
  Next Thursday.
2 When does your brother arrive?
  17th October.

Exercise 7

Listen

On the cassette you will hear answers to the following questions. *Tick* ☐ the correct answer **a**, **b** or **c**.

1	When are you going on holiday?	**a**	13th March	☐
		b	30th March	☐
		c	13th May	☐
2	When's your birthday?	**a**	Thursday 14th July	☐
		b	Tuesday 14th July	☐
		c	Thursday 4th July	☐
3	What's your date of birth, please?	**a**	5th September, 1960	☐
		b	15th September, 1916	☐
		c	15th September, 1960	☐
4	When do the exams begin?	**a**	Tuesday 13th June	☐
		b	Tuesday 30th June	☐
		c	Thursday 30th June	☐
5	Do you know when Shakespeare was born?	**a**	23rd April, 1654	☐
		b	21st April, 1564	☐
		c	23rd April, 1564	☐

7 Some numbers

Note

1 *Decimals* are normally written as follows: 3.25, and are said 'three *point* two five'.
2 *Fractions*: the most common are: ¼ 'a quarter', ½ 'a half', and ¾ 'three-quarters'.
3 *Ordinal numbers*: they are the same as those used in dates and are written and said as follows: 1st (first), 2nd (second), 3rd (third), 4th (fourth), 5th (fifth), 6th (sixth), etc. Numbers ending in 1 add 'st', those ending in 2 add 'nd', those ending in 3 add 'rd'; all others add 'th'.
    Example: 21st (twenty-first), 22nd (twenty-second), 23rd (twenty-third), 14th (fourteenth), 35th (thirty-fifth), 68th (sixty-eighth)

Exercise 8

On your cassette there is an interview between a reporter from a local English newspaper and a marathon runner, Jim, who has just finished running in the London marathon race.

While you are listening to the interview, write in the table on the next page the appropriate numbers for distance, time, etc. It is not necessary for you to understand every word in the interview.

Listen

Marathon race interview

Distance: miles	_____
kilometres	_____
Number of runners	_____
Jim's finishing position	_____
His position last year	_____
Winner's time	_____
Jim's time	_____
Record time	_____

Note: The London Marathon is a long-distance road race in the centre of London which started in 1981. It is held in the spring each year, and thousands of men and women enter for it.

8   Food: in a hotel or restaurant

Exercise 9

On your cassette you will hear a waiter asking a hotel guest for his/her order for breakfast. As you are listening to the order being given, *tick* the items that are ordered on the menu below. Read the menu before listening.

Listen

The Grand Hotel Breakfast Menu	*Tick here*
fruit juice: orange	☐
grapefruit	☐
pineapple	☐
cereal: cornflakes	☐
porridge	☐
cooked: fried egg and bacon	☐
scrambled egg and bacon. . . .	☐
fried egg, sausage and tomato	☐
boiled egg	☐
toast	☐
tea	☐
coffee	☐

Exercise 10

On your cassette you will hear a husband and wife discussing what to have for dinner in a restaurant. As you are listening to the discussion, *tick* the items that the *wife* chooses on the menu below. Read the menu before listening.

Listen

The Good Food Restaurant
Dinner Menu

Tick here

Starters	orange juice	☐
	melon.	☐
	egg mayonnaise.	☐
	prawn cocktail	☐
	tomato soup	☐
Main Course	grilled steak	☐
	roast beef	☐
	chicken and rice	☐
	fried plaice	☐
	mushroom omelette . . .	☐
Vegetables	peas	☐
	carrots	☐
	beans	☐
	chips.	☐
	boiled potatoes	☐
Sweet/Dessert	apple pie	☐
	caramel custard	☐
	chocolate cake.	☐
	ice cream.	☐
	fruit salad	☐
	cheese and biscuits. . . .	☐
Drinks	fruit juice.	☐
	beer	☐
	wine	☐
	coffee.	☐

35

9 Money: price and costs

Listen

i) The dialogues below are on your cassette.

a How much does this cost, please?
£3 exactly.

b What's the price of that dress, please?
£17.99.

'How much does this cost please?'
'£3 exactly.'

Note	British money has 100 pence (100p) = 1 pound (£1). £17.99 is seventeen pounds and ninety-nine pence, often said 'seventeen (pounds) ninety-nine'. The word 'pence' is often shortened to 'p', thus '10 pence' is often said 'ten p'.

Exercise 11

On your cassette you will hear two people talking, one is asking questions about prices, the other is answering.
Write in the spaces below the *price (in figures)* that is given as the answer to each question.

Listen

1 How much is that, please? _____

2 How much are those shoes, please? _____

3 How much is the bill, please? _____

4 What's the price of that second-hand car over there? _____

5 Can you tell me how much is left in my bank account, please? _____

6 What's the return fare to Bristol, please? _____

7 How much were the theatre tickets? _____

8 What will this cost to send by parcel post, please? _____

9 A dozen eggs and a pint of milk, please. _____

10 How much are those small cakes, please? _____

ii) On your cassette you will hear a short dialogue between a customer, John Bull, and a shopkeeper. The customer is paying his bill by cheque and is asking the shopkeeper who he should make the cheque payable to. As you are listening to the dialogue look at the cheque below which has been completed as an example. Notice that on the cheque sums of money are written in words and figures.

Listen

Exercise 12

On your cassette there is another dialogue between a customer and a shopkeeper. In the same way as in the example above, the customer, John Bull, is asking the shopkeeper about writing the cheque. As you are listening to the dialogue write in the cheque below the amount of money in words and figures, and also the date.

Listen

```
0                                            _____ 19____      00-00-00

        National Westminster Bank PLC
        Anytown Branch
        41 High Street, Anytown, Berks.

Pay _____                      or order
                                                  £ _____
    _____                      JOHN BULL

                                            John Bull

    ⑈123456⑈ 00⑈0000⑉ 999999999⑈
```

10 Telephoning

i) When giving or asking for telephone numbers, say each figure separately. However, when the same figures occur together at the beginning or end of a group, the word 'double' is used with the figure. The '0' is pronounced 'Oh' (i.e. the same as the letter 'O'). Read the following as you listen.

Listen

Is that 283 4465?
Yes. Can I help you?
I'd like to speak to Mr Jones, please.

Note

Titles normally used for people are:
Miss – for single women
Mrs   – for married women | or Ms for either
Mr   – for men
Dr   – for Doctor

Exercise 13

Write in the spaces below the *telephone numbers* and *names* that you hear in each dialogue. The dialogue is between a caller on the phone and a secretary.

Listen

1 Is that _____?

Yes. Can I help you?

I'd like to speak to

_____, please.

2 Is that _____?

Yes. Who do you want to speak to?

_____, please.

3 Is that _____?

Who do you wish to speak to?

_____, please.

The following are different from the above. A telephonist is answering the phone and saying the name of the organisation, and a caller is asking for an extension number. Write in the spaces below the *name of the organisation* and the *extension number*.

Listen

4 _____

Extension _____, please.

5 _____. Can I help you?

Extension _____, please.

6 _____

Extension _____, please.

ii) The following dialogue on the telephone is about *finding out a phone number*.

Listen

Operator: Directory Enquiries – which town?
Enquirer: Birmingham.
Operator: Name?
Enquirer: Green.
Operator: Initials, and the address?
Enquirer: A.K., 17 Queen's Road.
Operator: The number is 273 1469.

Note | You would need to add a 'dialling code' in front of the number for another town (for Birmingham it is 021-).

Exercise 14

Write in the spaces below the *places*, *names*, *addresses* and *phone numbers* that you hear.

Listen

1 *Operator:* Directory Enquiries. Which town?

Enquirer: _____

Operator: Name?

Enquirer: _____

Operator: Initials, and the address?

Enquirer: _____, 19 High Street.

Operator: The number is _____

2 *Operator:* Directory Enquiries. Which town?

Enquirer: _____

Operator: Name?

Enquirer: _____

Operator: Initials, and the address?

Enquirer: _____

Operator: The number is _____

3 *Operator:* Directory Enquiries. Which town?

   Enquirer: _____

   Operator: Name?

   Enquirer: _____

   Operator: Initials, and the address?

   Enquirer: _____

   Operator: The number is _____

iii) On your cassette you will hear a dialogue on the telephone between a secretary and a person who is making an appointment to see someone. While the person is speaking, the secretary makes a note of the appointment details. While you are listening to your cassette look at the secretary's note below.

Listen

```
Note for Mr Donaldson

        James   Smith

is coming to see you on

      Friday

at    12.15
```

Exercise 15

There are three more dialogues on your cassette. While you are listening, write the notes below for the secretary, to include the *name* of the person, the *day*, and the *time*.

Listen   **1**

```
Note for Professor Freeman

_____

is coming to see you on

_____

at _____
```

2

```
Note for Dr Nelson
_____

is coming to see you on
_____

at _____
```

3

```
Note for Mrs Harper
_____

is coming to see you on
_____

at _____
```

11   Accommodation

At a hotel
The following dialogue is on your cassette:

Listen

Visitor: Have you got a single room for one night, please?

Receptionist: Yes, *Room 124* on the *first floor*.

Visitor: How much is it?

Receptionist: *£12.50*, including breakfast.

If you were the visitor making a note of the information you might write as follows:

```
Room no.   124
Floor      1
Cost       £12.50
```

Exercise 16

On your cassette you will hear dialogues between a visitor to a hotel and the receptionist, similar to the example on page 41. As you are listening to the dialogues write in the boxes below the information about the *room number*, the *floor* and the *cost*.

Listen

1

Room no. _____

Floor _____

Cost _____

2

Room no. _____

Floor _____

Cost _____

3

Room no. _____

Floor _____

Cost _____

Renting a flat
On the cassette you will hear a dialogue between a person looking for a flat and the owner (or landlord) of the accommodation. The person looking for the flat has seen an advertisement and is telephoning the owner to find out more information about it. The person telephoning has made a note of the information on the next page. Look at it first and make sure you understand the headings on the left. Look at it again as you are listening to the cassette.

Listen

```
Accommodation information

Accommodation address  43 Hills Road, Exeter

Telephone no.  694 2258

Type of accommodation  furnished flat

No. of people suitable for  4 or 5

No. of bedrooms  3

Heating arrangements  gas central heating

Cooking arrangements  gas

Charge for accommodation  £90 a month

Vacant from  1st September
```

Exercise 17

In a similar way to the example you will hear a telephone dialogue between someone looking for a flat and the owner of it. As you are listening to the dialogue write notes on the information in the spaces below. Two items have already been filled in for you.

Listen

```
Accommodation information

Accommodation address  _____

Telephone no.  423 6197

Type of accommodation  furnished flat

No. of people suitable for  _____

No. of bedrooms  _____

Heating arrangements  _____

Cooking arrangements  _____

Charge for accommodation  _____

Vacant from  _____
```

Part 4 Describe and draw or label

In this part you will be listening to some dialogues and some descriptions. While you are listening you will be asked to either *draw* some of the information that you hear or to *write* in parts of a picture, plan or map.

1 People

On your cassette you will hear Tessa (a woman) talking to her friend John (a man), on the phone. She is asking him to describe three friends as she is going to meet them at the railway station and needs to be able to recognise them. While you are listening to the dialogue try to *draw* in the descriptions of the three men on the outline heads below. Under each head write the *height* that you hear (in centimetres).

Before you begin check that you understand the following words:

straight | hair   big   small   pointed | beard   moustache
curly   bald

Listen

Ken   Richard   Mike

2 A bicycle

You are going to listen to a description of the cleaning of a bicycle. Charles, a boy, always cleans the parts of his bike in the same order each time. The main parts are as follows (check that you understand them by looking at the small diagram).

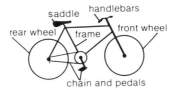

handlebars/front wheel/rear wheel/ chain and pedals/saddle/frame
(They are said at the beginning of the exercise on the cassette.)

As you are listening to the cleaning procedure, write the words from the list above in the correct boxes in the picture below. Write only those words; do *not* write other words that you will hear (it is not necessary to understand them). In the circle ◯ above each box write the *number* to indicate the order of cleaning that part. The first box and circle have been completed as an example.

Listen

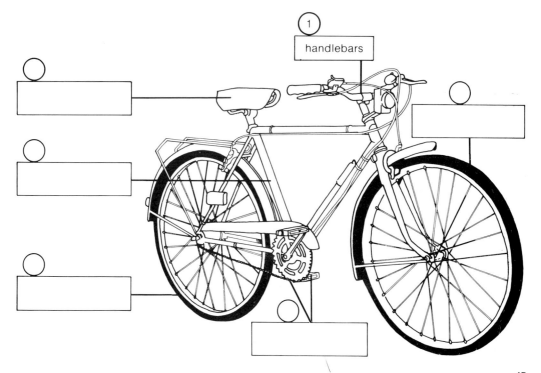

3 A block of flats

Below there is a diagram of a block of flats (or apartments). Each rectangular box in it represents a flat. On your cassette you will hear a dialogue between two men who deliver milk to the flats (milkmen). One of them is new to the milk round, and he is listening to the experienced milkman describing who lives in which flat. As you are listening to the milkmen speaking, write in the correct boxes the *names* of the occupants together with the *numbers* of their flats (in the corner of each flat). The names that you will hear are as follows:

Mr and Mrs Snow, Mr and Mrs Good, Miss Sally Green, Miss June Green, Mrs Jenkins, Mr Roberts, Mr Stone, Dr Peter Black.

Listen

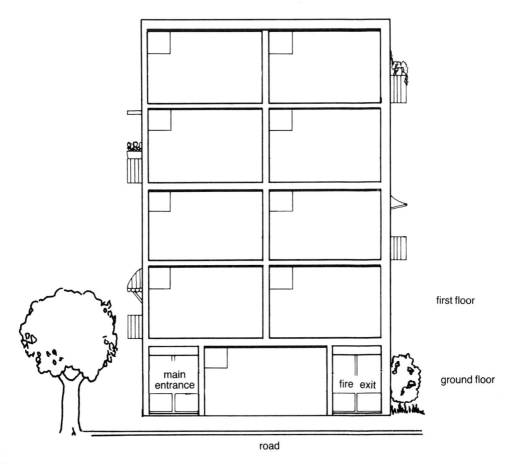

4 A street plan

Look carefully at the street plan below.

A On your cassette you will hear three separate sets of directions for walking to a particular place on the street plan of Moreton. As you are listening, follow the directions carefully on the plan. At the end of each set of directions there are some questions. Write the answers below. *The first one starts at the railway station.*

Listen

1 What is on your right? _____

2a Which road are you now in? _____

b What is the building on your left? _____

3 What is the building on your right? _____

B On your cassette you will hear a dialogue between two people. One of them is describing a route around the town of Moreton. On the street plan *draw a line* to show the route taken. If the person went *inside* any of the places named on the plan, mark that place with a cross ✕.

Listen

When you have finished, check your answers carefully.

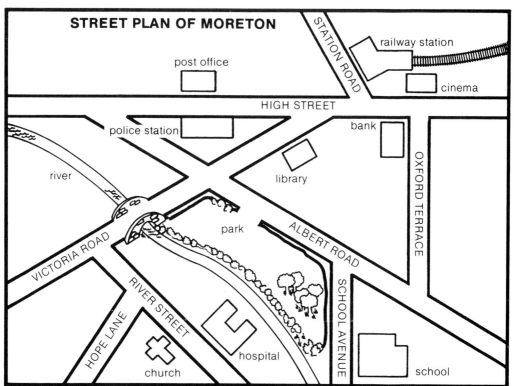

STREET PLAN OF MORETON

5   A route map

On your cassette you will hear a description on a local radio news
broadcast of a plane's flight around the UK. The plane lands at
several airports which are marked on the map below. While you
are listening to the flight description draw a line on the map to
show the route that the plane took. Put a cross ✕ through any
airport ▲ where the aeroplane *lands*. If you hear how long the
plane stops at any airport, write the time in figures next to the
airport name on the map. Look carefully at the map before you
listen. *The flight starts at Cardiff (South Wales).*

Listen

UNITED KINGDOM

(U.K. = England, Scotland,
Wales, Northern Ireland.)

KEY

▲ airport

Part 5 Comparing information

In this part you will hear some short descriptions: of an organisation, a place, a car, pet animals, and a person. You will be asked to compare the information that you *hear* with similar information that you *read*, and to underline the changes that have been made.

1 The Common Market

Read the text below at the same time as you are listening to it being read on your cassette. Some changes will be made to the text that is on the cassette. When you read any *words* or *numbers* that are different from those that you hear on the cassette, underline them.

Example: if the voice on the cassette said:
'. . . *consisted of seven member countries: Belgium, France, East Germany* . . .' and the text that you read has: '. . . *consisted of six member countries: Belgium, France, West Germany* . . .' then you should underline the differences, i.e. 'six ' and 'West'.

To help you – in this first text there will be 6 changes to listen for: the first two are in the first sentence . . .

Listen

The European Economic Community (or EEC), otherwise known as the Common Market, is a Western European economic association. It was set up by the Treaty of Rome in 1958, and originally consisted of six member countries: Belgium, France, West Germany, Holland, Italy and Luxembourg.

Britain, together with Ireland and Denmark, joined the Common Market on 1st January, 1973. Greece joined in 1980, thus making a total membership of ten countries. Since then Spain and Portugal have also applied for membership.

Note: If you have not found the six changes, listen again carefully.

2 Greater Manchester

Read the text below at the same time as you are listening to it being read on your cassette. Some changes will be made to the text that is on the cassette. When you read any *words* or *numbers* that are different from those that you hear on the cassette, underline them. To help you – there will be 7 changes to listen for: the first one is in the first sentence; the second one is in the second sentence . . .

Listen

Greater Manchester County is one of three major urban areas in the UK and the largest in North West England. It has a population of over 2.7 million, resident in an area of 500 square miles.

Traditional industries of the County have been coal mining and cotton manufacture and the industrial structure has been transformed in the last twenty years by the new industries of light engineering, transport and warehousing, although old crafts and skills still remain.

Greater Manchester is situated almost in the centre of the UK: 187 miles north of London and 213 miles south of Edinburgh. It is within 40 minutes journey by road of the cities of Leeds and Liverpool. London is only 2½ hours away by rail.

Note: If you have not found the seven changes, listen again carefully.

3 Ford Escort Car

Read the text below at the same time as you are listening to it being read on your cassette. Some changes will be made to the text that is on the cassette. When you read any *words* or *numbers* that are different from those that you hear on the cassette, underline them. To help you – there will be 9 changes to listen for . . .

Listen

One of the most popular British motor cars is the Ford Escort. It has a reputation for being an efficient, practical and economical car. In fact, in 1981, it was voted 'Car of the Year'.

One model has a 1300 c.c. engine and five doors. Four of the doors are at the sides for the driver and passengers, and the fifth is at the rear for luggage. The spare wheel is kept in the rear with the luggage. Some of the models contain a radio and a clock, as well as a cigarette lighter and the more usual interior heater.

The car will do between 30 and 50 miles

per gallon of petrol. The precise figure depends on the driving conditions and the speed. In 1982 the price of the car, depending on the particular model, varied between £4,000 and £5,750.

4 Pet animals

Read the text below at the same time as you are listening to it being read on your cassette. Some changes will be made to the text that is on the cassette. When you read any *words* or *numbers* that are different from those you hear on the cassette, or that have been left out, underline them.

Listen   You are not told the number of changes to listen for . . .

Many British families keep pets at home. Pets are tame animals that are kept in the home for different reasons, but mainly to provide companionship and amusement. The two main groups of people who like pets the most are children and elderly people.

From looking after their pets, boys and girls can learn the meaning of responsibility. This is particularly true if they are responsible for feeding the pets and cleaning out their cages or boxes. Probably the most popular pets are dogs and cats, but with children smaller animals are often more popular, for example, rabbits, guinea pigs, white mice, and sometimes caged birds.

Elderly people prefer dogs and cats as pets. They are easier to look after, and return affection. In particular, they provide companionship which can be very important for a person living alone.

5 D.H. Lawrence: English novelist and poet

This exercise is more difficult than the previous ones as it contains the names of people, places and books.

In the same way as the previous exercises, read the text below at the same time as you are listening to it being read on your cassette. Some changes will be made to the text that is on the cassette. When you read any *words* or *numbers* that are different from those that you hear on the cassette, or that have been left out, <u>underline</u> them.

Listen   You are not told the number of changes to listen for . . .

D.H. Lawrence

David Herbert Lawrence was born at Eastwood, near Nottingham, in 1885, the son of a coal miner. He was educated at Nottingham University College, where he qualified as a teacher. He taught at an elementary school in London until 1913 when he had to resign because of illness. After this he devoted himself to literature.

His first book, *The White Peacock* was published in 1911. In 1912 Lawrence went to Italy with Frieda, the wife of Professor Ernest Weekley. After Frieda's divorce, Lawrence married her in 1914. His first masterpiece, *Sons and Lovers* was published in 1913: in many places it is directly autobiographical. Other novels which are well-known are *The Rainbow*, *Women in Love*, and *Lady Chatterley's Lover*, published in 1928.

Lawrence died of tuberculosis near Nice in 1930.

Part 6 Information transfer

In this part you will hear a short talk and some interviews: all of them are longer pieces to listen to than in the last part. You will be asked to write some of the information that you hear, in a table or diagram, or to take some brief notes. It will not be necessary to understand every word that you hear.

1 Overseas students in the UK

While you are listening to the short talk on your cassette about overseas students in the UK, write what is necessary to complete the tables below. You will need to use some *numbers*, *names of countries*, *English cities*, and an *academic subject*. Before you begin look carefully at the tables below: notice the information that they contain and where the spaces are.

This exercise will give you practice in writing figures (which is not easy to do from listening). If necessary, stop the cassette while you are writing.

Listen

Table 1 Overseas students in the UK, 1980–81

Total	_____
Commonwealth*	
Total	_____
Malaysia	_____
Hong Kong	_____
_____	5,468
EEC	
Total	_____
France	_____
_____	3,010
Ireland	_____
Foreign Countries	
Total	_____
Iran	_____
	_____
Switzerland	_____

Table 2 Overseas students at university in 1980 (undergraduate and postgraduate)

Total students	_____
Universities with most students	
London	
Leeds	_____
_____	1,130
_____	
UMIST	_____
Most popular subjects	
Engineering and technology	_____
Social, administrative and business studies	_____

Note: **Commonwealth:* an association of independent states, which were formerly part of the British Empire (colonies and dominions); established to encourage trade and friendly relations among its members.

53

2 A secretary's day

On your cassette you will hear an interview with a secretary who works with a business organisation in a city centre. The interviewer is asking the secretary a number of questions about her working day, especially about the times when she does certain things.

At the same time as you are listening to the interview, write some of the details in the spaces on the diary page below. You will need to write *a time*, or *length of time*, or *a few words* to describe the activity. Look at the diary page first and see where the spaces are. Some of the items have already been completed.

Listen

Diary page

	Time	Activity
morning		get up
	7. 30 – 7. 50	
		leave home
	9. 30	
	11.00 –	
afternoon	–	lunch break
	3. 30 –	
		finish work
evening	6. 30	
		dinner

54

Penny Black

3 Stamp collecting: the world's greatest hobby

On your cassette you will hear an interview between a local newspaper reporter and Mr Gibbon, whose hobby is stamp collecting. Mr Gibbon is being asked a number of questions about his hobby. While you are listening to the interview, write some notes (a few words or numbers) in the spaces in the reporter's notebook below. Look at the notebook page first and make sure you understand the headings that are given.

Listen

Reporter's notebook

Mr Gibbon's hobby: stamp collecting
1   Age when he started collecting _____
2   Number of years collecting _____
3   First stamps _____
4   Size of stamp collection _____
5   Value of stamps _____
6   Oldest stamp _____
7   Countries collected _____
8   Themes/subjects collected _____
_____

55

4 The history of postal transport in Britain

On your cassette you will hear another interview between the local newspaper reporter and Mr Gibbon, the stamp collector. This time Mr Gibbon is being asked to describe developments in the methods of transporting letters, both inside Britain and from Britain to other countries. Sometimes, instead of using the word 'letters' Mr Gibbon uses 'the (Royal) mail'. As you are listening to the description, write some brief notes in the boxes in the diagram below. You should write a *date* first, followed by one or more words to describe the *method of carrying letters*. Look at the diagram: you will see that it has been started for you.

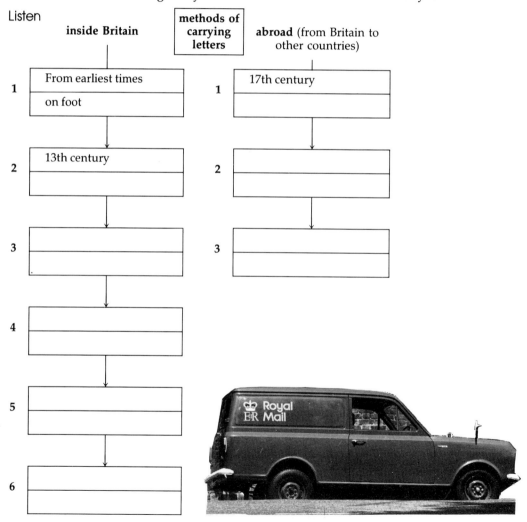

Listen

inside Britain   **methods of carrying letters**   **abroad** (from Britain to other countries)

1 | From earliest times | 1 | 17th century |
   | on foot |

2 | 13th century | 2 | |

3 | | 3 | |

4 | |

5 | |

6 | |

Answer key

Part 1 Sounds

1 The sounds of English

Note:

Group 1: These are *consonant sounds.*
Consonant sounds are made by partly or completely stopping the flow of air as it goes through the mouth.

Group 2: These are *vowel sounds.*
Vowel sounds are those in which the breath is let out without any stop or any closing of the air passage in the mouth or throat (that can be heard).

Group 3: These are *diphthong sounds.*
Diphthong sounds are compound vowel sounds made by pronouncing two vowel sounds quickly, one after the other.

Exercise 1

1	pea/pea √	6	sudden/southern ✗
2	fee/pea ✗	7	so/show ✗
3	pick/pig ✗	8	fished/fished √
4	vine/wine ✗	9	win/wing ✗
5	thick/thick √	10	led/red ✗

Exercise 2

1	sheep/ship ✗	6	could/could √
2	bed/bad ✗	7	but/bat ✗
3	cat/cart ✗	8	coat/coat √
4	got/goat ✗	9	down/done ✗
5	caught/caught √	10	here/hair ✗

2 Some pairs of sounds

Exercise 3

1	foot	8	could	15	hat
2	boat	9	prize	16	port
3	fan	10	she	17	four
4	town	11	cheap	18	hut
5	thin	12	leave	19	cup
6	they	13	bell	20	work
7	teeth	14	man		

Exercise 4

1	pat	5	march	8	rich
2	den	6	view	9	bed
3	sue	7	came	10	lock
4	bit				

Exercise 5

1a She is <u>living</u> with her brother. √
2b His <u>cap</u> was very dirty. √
3b Has the <u>bus</u> arrived yet? √
4b He <u>hid</u> the ball in the garden. √
5a What do you think of the <u>prices</u>? √

Note:
If there are difficulties in producing some of the *consonant sounds*, it may be helpful to group them in a different way for practice purposes. This may be done by dividing 16 of the consonant sounds into two groups: one group is *voiced* (meaning that the vocal cords in the throat vibrate for

a sound), and the other group is *voiceless* (meaning that the vocal cords do *not* vibrate – only breath comes out with the sound). It is possible to group the 16 sounds into 8 pairs: the articulation is the same for each sound in the pair, but one sound is voiced, the other voiceless.

8 pairs of consonant sounds

voiceless		voiced	
phonetic symbol	sound underlined in word	phonetic symbol	sound underlined in word
/p/	pat	/b/	bat
/t/	ten	/d/	den
/k/	came	/g/	game
/tʃ/	rich	/dʒ/	ridge
/f/	few	/v/	view
/θ/	teeth	/ð/	teethe
/s/	sue	/z/	zoo
/ʃ/	Confucian	/ʒ/	confusion

Note: The only other *voiceless* sound in English is /h/ as in hot; all other sounds are voiced.

Exercise 6   Dictation
(Correct alternatives are included in brackets.)

1	pen	6	live	11	bat	16	bad
2	ten	7	march	12	day	17	lock
3	key (quay)	8	saw (sore, soar)	13	could	18	hut
4	cheap (cheep)	9	work	14	foot	19	game
5	thin	10	now	15	she	20	there (their)

Note: If you get any wrong, listen again carefully. If necessary, listen again to 1 *The sounds of English.*

3   Some sounds at the ends of words

Note:

a *The pronunciation of the letters 's' or 'es' at the end of a word*
When the plural of a word, or a possessive, or the third person singular of the (active) present simple tense of a verb, ends in the letters 's' or 'es', three different pronunciations are possible. The choice of the final sound /s/, /z/, /ɪz/ is determined by the final sound of the word before the letter 's' (or 'es') is added.
1   When a word ends in one of the following sounds /s/, /z/, /ʃ/, /tʃ/, /dʒ/, /ʒ/, and then 's' or 'es' is added, the pronunciation of the 's' or 'es' will be /ɪz/.
2   When a word ends in a *voiced* consonant sound (see the note for 2 *Some pairs of sounds* above) – other than those in **1** above – or a vowel or diphthong sound, and then 's' or 'es' is added, the pronunciation or the 's' or 'es' will be /z/.

3 When a word ends in one of the following *voiceless* consonant sounds /f/, /p/, /t/, /k/, /θ/, and then 's' or 'es' is added, the pronunciation of the 's' or 'es' will be /s/.

Note: Some examples of irregularities: Notice how the sound before /ɪz/ or /z/ changes.

hou<u>se</u>	/s/	hou<u>ses</u>	/zɪz/
pa<u>th</u>	/θ/	pa<u>ths</u>	/ðz/

b *The pronunciation of the letters 'ed' at the end of a word*
When the past tense of a verb ends in the letters 'ed', there are three possible ways to pronounce the ending: /ɪd/, /t/, /d/. The choice of the final sound is determined by the final sound of the word before the letters 'ed' are added.
1 When a verb ends in the sound /t/ or /d/ the pronunciation of the letters 'ed' will be /ɪd/.
2 When a verb ends in a *voiceless* consonant sound except /t/, (see the note for *2 Some pairs of sounds* above), the pronunciation of the letters 'ed' will be /t/.
3 When a verb ends in a vowel, diphthong, or *voiced* consonant sound, except /d/, the pronunciation of the letters 'ed' will be /d/.

Note: All adjectives ending in 'ed' and adverbs ending in 'edly' are pronounced /ɪd/ and /ɪdlɪ/ respectively.
Example: wick<u>ed</u> /ɪd/   wick<u>edly</u> /ɪdlɪ/.

Exercise 7

Group **a** – /s/	Group **b** – /z/	Group **c** – /ɪz/
eats	lives	watches
coughs	beds	bridges
kicks	says	dishes
	boys	

Exercise 8

Group **a** – /t/	Group **b** – /d/	Group **c** – /ɪd/
worked	closed	wanted
pushed	opened	demanded
kissed	climbed	
	played	
	hired	

4   Contractions

Exercise 9
1b You'll hear. √
2b They're ready. √
3b She'd go. √
4a I've written. √

Exercise 10
1b They weren't going. √
2a I shan't get it. √

3a You haven't done it. √
4b He wouldn't do it. √

Exercise 11a
1b She's sitting on the floor. √
2a She walked every day. √
3b We'll finish it later. √
4b He hasn't received the money. √
5b I'd buy it for you. √
6a She isn't like her father. √
7a They don't want the books. √
8a It was a glass. √
9b They can't do it. √
10b He wasn't washing up. √

Exercise 11b
1 He is.
2 She has.
3 I should/would.

Exercise 12

1a	They robbed a bank	different	√
b	They've robbed a bank.		
2a	She said she did it.	different	√
b	She said she didn't.		
3a	They look at TV nearly every day.	different	√
b	They looked at TV nearly every day.		
4a	They listen to the radio every day.	same	√
b	They listen to the radio every day.		
5a	He's planning a good one.	different	√
b	His plan is a good one.		

5   Singular and plural

Exercise 13   Dictation
1   These questions are very difficult.
2   Those papers were the wrong ones.
3   This advice is very sensible.
4   She didn't listen to the news.
5   He was given some information on it.
6   He thinks it was another one.
7   There was a little water in the glass.
8   She says he means the other book.

Part 2   Stress and intonation

1   Short stress patterns

Exercise 1

	— ●		● —		— ●
1	tell her	5	a book	8	help him
2	the desk	6	we'll try	9	send it
3	it's old	7	his shoes	10	he's in
4	got it				

Exercise 2

a — ●	b ● —
sell it	they walk
read them	she's out
	he knows

2   Longer stress patterns

Exercise 3
1   We travelled by train.
2   A cup of coffee.
3   He'll give you another one.
4   She hasn't been before.
5   You're wanted on the phone.

3   Noun stress

Exercise 4

— ●	— ● ●
college	lecturer
English	principal
sentence	paragraph
essay	holiday
travel	
ticket	

4   Variable stress

Exercise 5

● — ● ●	● — ● ●	● ● — ● ●
4b industrial	5b political	6b agricultural

5   Verb stress

Exercise 6

Pattern 1 — ●	*Pattern 2* ● —
brighten	advise
punish	promote
shorten	believe
polish	translate
	receive
	excuse

Note:

1 *Two-syllable verbs* beginning with the following elements have the strong stress on the *second* syllable (● ——).

ad-	en-	re-
be-	im-	sub-
com-	in-	suc-
con-	mis-	trans-
de-	out-	ob-
dis-	pro-	un-
em-	pre-	with-

2 *Verb suffix '-ate'*
In verbs ending with '-ate', the stress is on '-ate' if the verb has two syllables, but it is on the third syllable from the end if the verb is longer than two syllables.

Example: relate   operate   congratulate

3 *Verb suffixes '-ize' or '-ise'*
In verbs of three or more syllables ending with '-ize(-ise)', the stress is usually three syllables from the end.

Example: exercise   industrialize

6 Noun and verb stress

Exercise 7

1 Terry will *record* your voice on tape.

2 Metals *contract* when the temperature falls.

3 These goods are for *export* only.

4 She's making good *progress* in English.

5 Prices continue to *increase* each year.

Exercise 8

1	protest	6	accent
2	present	7	survey
3	desert	8	produce
4	transport	9	subject
5	object	10	frequent

7 Significant stress

Exercise 9

1 Did Tony buy that <u>black</u> car?
2 Did <u>Tony</u> buy that black car?
3 Did Tony buy <u>that</u> black car?
4 Did Tony <u>buy</u> that black car?

Exercise 10a

a	'273 3095.'	'Sorry, I wanted 273 30<u>8</u>5.'	8
b	'126 2812.'	'Sorry, I wanted 126 1<u>8</u>12.'	1
c	'653 7285.'	'Sorry, I wanted 6<u>4</u>3 7285.'	4
d	'27634.'	'Sorry, I wanted 2763<u>5</u>.'	5
e	'409 3417.'	'Sorry, I wanted 409 <u>2</u>417.'	2
f	'57981.'	'Sorry, I wanted 57<u>0</u>81.'	0

Exercise 10b

a	'Sorry, I wanted 80<u>4</u> 1213.'	4
b	'Sorry, I wanted 372 <u>4</u>061.'	4
c	'Sorry, I wanted 507982.'	2
d	'Sorry, I wanted 435 <u>7</u>957.'	7
e	'Sorry, I wanted 7<u>6</u>0 0846.'	6
f	'Sorry, I wanted 193 52<u>7</u>4.'	7

8 Essential weak stress forms

Exercise 11

1	He <u>was</u> late.	weak	/wəz/
2	She <u>must</u> go.	strong	/mʌst/
3	Look at <u>her</u>.	weak	/hə/
4	Where <u>does</u> he live?	weak	/dəz/
5	They <u>have</u> lost it.	strong	/hæv/

Exercise 12
1 She says <u>that</u> <u>he</u> <u>has</u> got one.
2 A dog ran out of the house.
3 He <u>was</u> older <u>than</u> <u>the</u> others.
4 There <u>were</u> <u>a</u> lot <u>from</u> <u>the</u> other school.
5 Give it <u>to</u> <u>them</u> <u>as</u> soon <u>as</u> possible.

Exercise 13
1 Where <u>has</u> <u>he</u> gone?
2 They <u>are</u> brother <u>and</u> sister.
3 Give <u>them</u> another week <u>to</u> finish.
4 I asked <u>her</u> <u>to</u> buy <u>me</u> <u>some</u> bread.
5 He said <u>that</u> <u>he</u> <u>can</u> do it.
6 What <u>have</u> they got <u>to</u> do?
7 When <u>can</u> she call <u>for</u> a new one?
8 He <u>was</u> away <u>from</u> work last week.

9 Intonation patterns

Exercise 14
[↗] him?   [↘] yes.   [↘] mine.
[↗] whose?   [↘] wait.   [↘] right.

Exercise 15
1 Why are you so ˋlate?
2 Must you ˏgo now?
3 Are you ˏhappy?
4 He'll be along ˋlater.
5 Do you mind if I ˏsmoke?
6 How far is it to ˋLondon?

Exercise 16
1 ˏYes?   question
2 ˏHere?   question
3 ˋThese.   statement
4 ˏFive?   question
5 ˋMe.   statement

Note:
The information on intonation patterns (rising and falling) has been simplified. In practice, a number of patterns are used which modify the two main types. These modifications may cause different amounts of rise or fall in different parts of the sentence. However, this can be rather complicated. The purpose of the exercises here is to help to develop an awareness of intonation patterns. The variations in the patterns may be noticed in Part 3.

Part 3   Practical dialogues

1   The letters of the alphabet

Note: The *vowel* letters in the English alphabet are: **a**, **e**, **i**, **o**, **u**. All the other letters are *consonants*.

Exercise 1

1	G	2	E	3	P	4	I	5	M
6	A	7	C	8	J	9	R	10	W

2   Some common abbreviations

Note: The abbreviations given in your workbook stand for the following:

1	BBC	British Broadcasting Corporation
2	EEC	European Economic Community
3	GB	Great Britain
4	ILO	International Labour Organisation
5	SOS	save our souls = help
6	UK	United Kingdom (of Great Britain and Northern Ireland)
7	UN	United Nations
8	USA	United States of America
9	USSR	Union of Soviet Socialist Republics
10	WHO	World Health Organisation

Exercise 2

1	AGM	2	GMT	3	HQ	4	IMF
5	NB	6	PS	7	PTO	8	IOU
9	TUC	10	VHF				

Note: These abbreviations are explained below.

1	AGM	Annual General Meeting
2	GMT	Greenwich Mean Time
3	HQ	Headquarters
4	IMF	International Monetary Fund
5	NB	Nota Bene (Latin = note carefully)
6	PS	Postscript = a note at the end of a letter
7	PTO	Please turn over (written at the bottom of a page)
8	IOU	I owe you (some money)
9	TUC	Trades Union Congress
10	VHF	very high frequency

3   Form-filling: personal information

Secretary: Good morning. Can I help you?
Student: Yes, I'd like to enrol for the course?
Secretary: Certainly . . . what's your surname please?
Student: SVENSSON.
Secretary: Could you spell that for me?
Student: Yes, it's S-V-E-N-S-S-O-N.
Secretary: Thank you . . . and what's your first name?
Student: ARVID. That's spelled A-R-V-I-D.
Secretary: Thanks. Where are you from Mr Svensson?
Student: Sweden.
Secretary: I see. So your mother tongue is Swedish, isn't it?
Student: Yes, that's right.
Secretary: How old are you?
Student: 40.
Secretary: Thank you.

Exercise 3

Secretary: Good afternoon. Can I help you?
Student: Yes, I'd like to enrol for the course.
Secretary: Certainly . . . what's your surname please?
Student: HANSEN.
Secretary: Could you spell that for me?
Student: Yes, it's H-A-N-S-E-N.
Secretary: Thank you . . . and what's your first name?
Student: LARS. That's spelled L-A-R-S.
Secretary: Thanks. Where are you from Mr Hansen?
Student: Denmark.
Secretary: I see. So your mother tongue is Danish, isn't it?
Student: Yes, that's right.
Secretary: How old are you?
Student: 28.
Secretary: Thank you.

Surname   **HANSEN**
(in CAPITAL LETTERS)

First name *Lars*

Male/female (underline as appropriate)

Country   *Denmark*

Mother tongue *Danish*

Age   *28*

4 Time

Exercise 4

1 Excuse me. Can you tell me the time, please?
   Yes, it's a quarter to one.

2 Do you have the right time, please?
   I think it's half past eleven.

3 Do you know what time the next bus is, please?
   Yes, it's twenty to twelve.

4 When do the shops open, please?
   At nine o'clock.

5 What time does the film finish, please?
   Ten past seven.

6 What time do you finish work today?
   Twenty past five.

7 When did she arrive?
   At twenty-five to three?

8 Must you go now?
   Yes, it's already five to eight.

9 Do you know when the play finishes?
   Yes, at exactly twenty-five past ten.

5 Time and travel

Exercise 5

1 What time does the Southampton train leave, please?
   11.13 (eleven thirteen).
2 What's the next train to Glasgow, please?
   12.50 (twelve fifty).
3 Excuse me, please. What time does the Bristol train arrive?
   14.40 (fourteen forty).
4 When does the Tokyo flight leave, please?
   22.15 (twenty-two fifteen).
5 What time's the next flight to Oslo, please?
   17.30 (seventeen thirty).

Note: Notice carefully the difference in pronunciation of numbers ending in '-teen' compared with '-ty' e.g. 14 (four<u>teen</u>) and 40 (for<u>ty</u>).

Exercise 6

1 The train now standing at <u>Platform 2</u> is the <u>15.40</u> to <u>Birmingham</u>.
2 The next train to arrive at <u>Platform 4</u> is the <u>9.50</u> to <u>London</u>.
3 The express train to <u>Liverpool</u> is now due in on <u>Platform 5</u> at <u>16.15</u>.
4 The next train to <u>Oxford</u> will depart from <u>Platform 3</u> at <u>11.42</u>.
5 British Rail apologises for the delay to the <u>Cambridge</u> train. It will now depart at <u>2.14</u> from <u>Platform 1</u>.
6 British Airways announces the departure of <u>Flight BA 107</u> at <u>14.30</u> to <u>Athens</u>.
7 British Airways next flight to <u>Paris</u> is Flight <u>BA 962</u> at <u>08.35</u>.
8 SAS Flight <u>SK 513</u> to <u>Stockholm</u> will depart at <u>19.55</u>.
9 Olympic Airways <u>Flight OA 593</u> for <u>Athens</u> will depart at <u>18.40</u>.

10 KLM, Royal Dutch Airlines, regrets the delay to <u>Flight KL 307</u> for <u>Amsterdam</u>. It will now depart at <u>17.25</u>.

	Platform number	Time	Destination
1	2	15.40	Birmingham
2	4	9.50	London
3	5	16.15	Liverpool
4	3	11.42	Oxford
5	1	2.14	Cambridge

	Flight number	Time	Destination
6	BA 107	14.30	Athens
7	BA 962	08.35	Paris
8	SK 513	19.55	Stockholm
9	OA 593	18.40	Athens
10	KL 307	17.25	Amsterdam

6 Dates

Exercise 7

1b 30th March
2b Tuesday 14th July
3c 15th September, 1960.
4a Tuesday 13th June
5c 23rd April, 1564.

7 Some numbers

Exercise 8

An interview with a marathon runner

Reporter: Hello Jim. I'm from your local newspaper the 'Weekly Post' and I'd like to ask you a few questions about the London marathon race that you've just finished.

Jim: That's all right. What would you like to know?

Reporter: Firstly, for the benefit of our readers, exactly how long is the marathon?

Jim: It's 26 miles 385 yards, or if you'd like it in metric it's 42.195 kilometres.

Reporter: Thanks. Now how many runners were there altogether?

Jim: More than ever this year . . . there were 16,417.

Reporter: My goodness, that's a lot! What position did you finish in the race Jim?

Jim: Well, I'm quite pleased with my performance. I came 2,014th.

Reporter: That's better than last year, isn't it?

Jim: Yes, I finished 3,470th then – but it was my first effort.

Reporter: By the way, what time did the race start today?

Jim: 9 o'clock. And the winner finished at 11.30.

Reporter: So he took 2½ hours. That's excellent. How long did you take?

Jim: 3¾ hours – but I know I can do better. Did you know that the record is 2 hours 10 minutes?

Reporter: I didn't know. That's fantastic! Do you know how long the slowest runner took?

Jim: No . . . he hasn't finished yet!

Distance: miles	26, and 385 yards
kilometres	42.195
Number of runners	16,417
Jim's finishing position	2,014th
His position last year	3,470th
Winner's time	2½ hours
Jim's time	3¾ hours
Record time	2 hours 10 minutes

8 Food: in a hotel or restaurant

Exercise 9

Waiter: Good morning. Can I take your order for breakfast?

Guest: Yes, thank you. I think I'll start with some grapefruit juice, followed by cornflakes.

Waiter: Yes . . . Would you like anything cooked to follow?

Guest: Yes, please. I'd like some scrambled egg and bacon. And afterwards I'd like some toast and marmalade.

Waiter: Very good. Would you like tea . . . or coffee?

Guest: I'll have coffee, please.

Note: Make sure that on the *Hotel Breakfast Menu* you have ticked the items underlined above.

Exercise 10

Husband: There's quite a good choice on the menu, isn't there dear?

Wife: Yes, but you know I always find it difficult to choose.

Husband: Well I've already decided what to have. We can order when you've made up your mind. What are you going to have to start with?

Wife: I fancy melon . . . but I can't decide whether to have chicken and rice or fried plaice . . . Oh, I remember, . . . I had fish the last time we were here, so I'll try the chicken and rice . . . and, let me see . . . yes, and some peas.

Husband: What about the sweet?

Wife: Well, we can order that later, but I think I'll have some fruit salad.

Husband: Shall I order some white wine to go with the meal?

Wife: Yes, that would be nice. By the way, what are you going to have?

Husband: Exactly the same as you!

Note: Make sure that on the *Restaurant Menu* you have ticked the items underlined above.

9 Money: price and costs

Exercise 11

1 That'll be 70 pence, please.
2 That pair is £18.50.

3 It comes to £13.89 altogether.
4 That one is just £840, sir.
5 Just a moment . . . yes, it's exactly £326.41.
6 The day return is £14.50.
7 Only £2.30 each.
8 Let me see . . . it'll be £1.73.
9 Thank you. That'll be 91p.
10 Oh, those? They're 40p each.

Customer: How would you like the cheque made out?
Shopkeeper: Make it payable to A.P. Black, if you would.
Customer: What was the total again?
Shopkeeper: It comes to seventeen pounds eighty-three (£17.83).
Customer: Oh yes.
Shopkeeper: Don't forget it's the first of July today.
Customer: Right. Thanks.

Exercise 12
Customer: How would you like the cheque made out?
Shopkeeper: Oh, please make it payable to B.R. Lyons – that's L-Y-O-N-S.
Customer: What did you say the total was?
Shopkeeper: It comes to fifteen pounds sixty-four (£15.64).
Customer: Oh yes.
Shopkeeper: Don't forget it's the first of March today.
Customer: Oh yes. So it is.

Note: Make sure that on the cheque you have written the items underlined above.

10 Telephoning

Exercise 13
1 Is that 407 3812?
   Yes. Can I help you?
   I'd like to speak to Miss Smith, please.
2 Is that 592 6433?
   Yes. Who do you want to speak to?
   Barbara Turner, please.
3 Is that 680 5717?
   Who do you wish to speak to?
   Dr Smart, please.
4 British Rail.
   Extension 19, please.

5 London University. Can I help you?
   Extension 9300, please.
6 British Council.
   Extension 342, please.

Exercise 14
1 *Operator:* Directory Enquiries. Which town?
   Enquirer: Leeds.
   Operator: Name?
   Enquirer: Frost?
   Operator: Initials, and the address?
   Enquirer: B.J. . . . 19 High Street.
   Operator: The number is 837 5029.

Note: The dialling code for Leeds is 0532.

2 *Operator:* Directory Enquiries. Which town?
   Enquirer: York.
   Operator: Name?
   Enquirer: White.
   Operator: Initials, and the address?
   Enquirer: D.M. . . . 130 King's Road.
   Operator: The number is 483 7706.

Note: The dialling code for York is 0904.

3 *Operator:* Directory Enquiries. Which town?
   Enquirer: Brighton.
   Operator: Name?
   Enquirer: James.
   Operator: Initials, and the address?
   Enquirer: W.E. . . . 43 Church Street.
   Operator: The number is 065 3287.

Note: The dialling code for Brighton is 0273.

iii) *Secretary:* Hello! Mr Donaldson's secretary. Can I help you?
    Enquirer: Good morning. I'd like to make an appointment to see Mr Donaldson on Friday, please.
    Secretary: Who's speaking please?
    Enquirer: James Smith.
    Secretary: Yes, Mr Smith. Friday is all right. Would 12.15 be convenient?
    Enquirer: Thank you. That'll be fine.

Exercise 15
1 *Secretary:* Hello. Professor Freeman's secretary. Can I help you?

Enquirer: Good afternoon. I'd like to make an appointment to see the professor on <u>Thursday</u>, please.
Secretary: Who's speaking please?
Enquirer: <u>Richard Jones</u>.
Secretary: Yes, Mr Jones. Would <u>9.45</u> be convenient?
Enquirer: Thank you. That'll be fine.

2 *Secretary:* Good morning. Dr Nelson's secretary. Can I help you?
Enquirer: Good morning. I'd like to make an appointment to see the doctor on <u>Wednesday</u>, please.
Secretary: Who's speaking please?
Enquirer: <u>Ann(e) Brown</u>.
Secretary: Thank you. Is <u>2.40</u> any good?
Enquirer: That's fine. Thank you very much.

3 *Secretary:* Hello. Can I help you?
Enquirer: I'd like to see Mrs Harper on <u>Tuesday</u>, please.
Secretary: Who's speaking please?
Enquirer: <u>David Sim</u>.
Secretary: Yes, it'll have to be in the afternoon. Will <u>4.20</u> do?
Enquirer: That'll be fine. Many thanks.

Note: Make sure that in the notes you have written the items underlined above.

11   Accommodation

At a hotel

Exercise 16
1 *Visitor:* Have you a double room for three nights, please?
Receptionist: Yes, you can have Room <u>207</u> on the <u>second</u> floor.
Visitor: How much does it cost, please?
Receptionist: <u>£18</u> a night, including a private bath.

2 *Visitor:* Can I book a single room for the weekend, please?
Receptionist: Yes, we have a room vacant on the <u>third</u> floor, <u>number 315</u>.
Visitor: What does it cost?
Receptionist: <u>£10.75</u> a night, including breakfast and service.

3 *Visitor:* Have you got a single room for one week, please?
Receptionist: Yes, Room <u>418</u>. It's on the <u>fourth</u> floor.
Visitor: How much is it?
Receptionist: <u>£14</u> a night, including English breakfast.

Note: Make sure that in the notes you have written the items underlined above.

Renting a flat

Owner: <u>694 2258</u>.
Enquirer: May I speak to the owner please?
Owner: Speaking.
Enquirer: Good afternoon. I've just seen the advertisement in the paper about the furnished flat to rent. Is it still available?
Owner: Yes, it is. Would you like to know something about it?
Enquirer: Yes, but could you tell me the address first please?
Owner: Yes, it's number <u>43 Hills Road, Exeter</u>.
Enquirer: Thank you. How big is the flat.
Owner: Oh, it's big enough for a family of <u>four or five</u>. There are <u>three</u> good-size <u>bedrooms</u>.
Enquirer: Thanks. What about the heating and cooking?
Owner: It's all <u>by gas</u> – the <u>central heating</u> and the <u>cooking</u>.
Enquirer: Right . . . and how much is the rent please?
Owner: It's <u>£90</u> a month, excluding the cost of the gas . . . The flat'll be available from the <u>beginning of September</u>.
Enquirer: Thank you very much . . .

Exercise 17
Owner: <u>423 6197</u>.
Enquirer: Hello. Is that Mr Johnson?
Owner: Yes, speaking.
Enquirer: I'm phoning about your advertisement in today's paper about the <u>furnished flat</u> you have to rent. Is it still available?
Owner: Yes it is, although somebody else has already phoned about it.
Enquirer: Could you tell me the address please?
Owner: Yes, it's <u>17 Green Street, York</u>.
Enquirer: Thank you. How many <u>bedrooms</u> has the flat got?

Owner: <u>Two</u>. They're quite big and would easily take <u>four people</u>.

Enquirer: I see. What are the heating and cooking arrangements.

Owner: Well, there are <u>electric fires</u> in all the rooms, and cooking is by <u>electricity</u> as well.

Enquirer: Thank you. How much is the rent please?

Owner: It's <u>£80 a month</u>. The <u>electricity is extra</u> and is on a meter.

Enquirer: If I rent the flat when would I be able to move in?

Owner: It's vacant from <u>1st October</u>, so any time after that.

Enquirer: Thank you . . .

Accommodation information

Accommodation address __17 Green Street, York__

Telephone no. __423 6197__

Type of accommodation __furnished flat__

No. of people suitable for __4__

No. of bedrooms __2__

Heating arrangements __electric fires__

Cooking arrangements __electricity__

Charge for accommodation __£80 a month__

Vacant from __1st October__

Part 4 Describe and draw or label

1 People

The dialogue is given first (important features underlined) followed by the drawings of the three heads.

John: 4367.

Tessa: Hello, John! I was just ringing to ask about your three friends. You asked me to meet them at the station tomorrow afternoon but you forgot to tell me what they look like! How will I recognise them?

John: Oh sorry, Tessa. Yes. Well . . . they're all very different from each other. Let's start with <u>Ken</u>. He's the oldest of the three. He's also the tallest, being about <u>190 cm</u>. You'll like him. He has <u>black curly hair</u> and a <u>small pointed beard</u>.

Tessa: Right! What about the next one?

John: <u>Richard's</u> the opposite of Ken in many ways. He's very short – about <u>155 cm</u>. He's almost completely <u>bald</u>: he's only got <u>a little hair at the sides above each ear</u>. But he does have <u>a big brown beard</u>.

Tessa: Thanks. And the third one?

John: <u>Mike</u> is medium height, about <u>170 cm</u>. He has <u>short, straight black hair</u> and <u>a small, thin moustache</u>. By the way, <u>he's always smoking a pipe: it's never out of his mouth!</u> One more thing I forgot. <u>Ken</u> is very short-sighted and <u>wears glasses</u>.

Tessa: Thanks a lot. I'll see them at 2 o'clock tomorrow.

John: Thanks, Tessa.

Tessa: Goodbye.

John: 'Bye.

Ken   190cm.   Richard   155cm.   Mike   170cm.

2 A bicycle

The description of the cleaning procedure is given first (important parts underlined) followed by the picture of the bicycle with the parts labelled in sequence. (The main parts of the bike are said as follows: *handlebars, front wheel, rear wheel, chain and pedals, saddle, frame*.)

Charles is always very thorough when he cleans his bike. He always cleans the parts carefully and in the same order each time so that he doesn't forget anything. Now listen to him describe the way he cleans his bike:

First I polish the <u>handlebars</u>, including the brakes, gears, the bell, and the front lamp. Secondly, I wash the bicycle <u>frame</u>, including the crossbar and the pump, but not the forks. I always find the frame quite easy because it never gets very dirty. Then I wipe the <u>saddle</u>. That's also easy because it only gets a little dusty underneath. After that I wash the <u>front wheel</u>, including the forks, mudguard, and spokes. It always takes quite a long time to clean the wheel properly because there are so many spokes to do. Then I clean the <u>chain and</u>

pedals and the chainguard. This is probably the dirtiest job of all as there's always a lot of dirt and grease on the chain. Finally, I wash the rear wheel, including the forks, mudguard, rear lamp, and the carrier. That always takes a long time to clean properly, just like the front wheel, and I'm always glad when it's finished . . . but it's all worth it because the bike looks really shiny when I've finished.

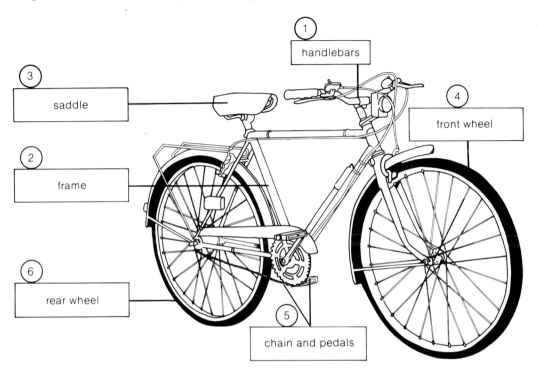

1 handlebars

3 saddle

2 frame

6 rear wheel

4 front wheel

5 chain and pedals

3 A block of flats

The dialogue between the two milkmen is given first (with the names of the occupants and the numbers of the flats underlined), followed by the completed diagram of the block of flats.

Bill: Right, let's start with the ground floor. This is number 1, and Mr Stone lives there – he's the caretaker. He's been looking after the flats for the last ten years. There's the main entrance on one side of his flat, and that's the fire exit on the other.
Now, immediately above him live two elderly sisters, who have a flat each. Miss Sally Green lives in the flat above the main entrance, that's number 2, and her sister, Miss June Green, lives above the fire exit, in number 3.

Ken: Right. I've got that so far. Mr Stone, Miss Sally Green and Miss June Green.

Bill: That's it. Now . . . above Sally Green is Dr Peter Black – he works in the local health centre . . . and above him live a retired couple, Mr and Mrs Good.

Ken: What number's Dr Black? Is it 4?

Bill: Yes, and Mr and Mrs Good are number 6. Now, coming back to the second floor, above June Green we've got the Snow family – Mr and Mrs Snow and their two children who both go to school. They're in number 5. OK?

71

Ken: Right. Who's next to Mr and Mrs Good?

Bill: In number <u>7</u> we've got <u>Mr Roberts</u>, a local bank manager.

Ken: And I think you said the flat above him is <u>empty</u>, isn't it?

Bill: That's right, that's number <u>9</u> . . . and next to that lives <u>Mrs Jenkins</u>, who's a widow. Her husband only died three months ago. She's living on her own.

Ken: That's number <u>8</u>, I suppose. Now let's see if I can remember: immediately below Mrs Jenkins are Mr and Mrs Good, and next to them is Mr Roberts . . .

Bill: All right, all right . . . I'm sure you know them all!

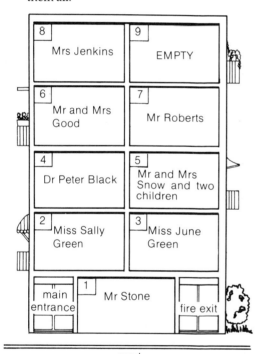

road

4 A street plan

A The sets of directions are listed below, with the questions and answers at the end of each one.

1 You've just come out of the railway station into Station Road. You face left and walk towards the High Street. You then turn right into the High Street. Take the first turning on your left and, after walking a little way, again take the first turning on your left. Walk straight on and you'll soon come to the entrance to something on your right.

What is on your right?   *Answer:* The park

2 You've just come out of the railway station into Station Road. You face left and walk towards the High Street. You then turn left into the High Street, cross over the street and, continuing in the same direction, take the first turning on your right. When you come to the end of that road, turn right, and then take the first on the left.

  a Which road are you now in?
    Answer: School Avenue
  b What is the building on your left?
    Answer: The school

3 You come out of the police station and, turning left, walk up the High Street. Take the turning on your left and at the cross-roads turn right. Walk straight on until you come to a road on your left. Turn into this road and walk straight along it, going past a turning on your right.

What is the building on your right?
Answer: The church

B The dialogue is as follows. The *route taken* and the *places visited* are marked on the plan under the dialogue.

Alan: Hello, Mary. Didn't I see you shopping in Moreton yesterday?

Mary: Yes, I was shopping. Well . . . not just shopping actually. I was so busy yesterday I thought I'd never finish.

Alan: Why, what happened?

Mary: Oh! It was just one of those days. After the shopping I had so many things to do . . . first of all I had to go to the <u>Post Office</u> to send a parcel off to my mother. Then on the way to the <u>bank</u> to cash a cheque I had to call in the library to return some overdue books. After that I had to call in at Brian's school to see his teacher for a few minutes.

Alan: Yes . . . you do seem to have been busy!

Mary: That wasn't the end of it! When I'd finished at the school I had to go back the way I'd come, to the cinema to try and book seats for tomorrow. But I found it was closed.

Alan: Oh no! Mary!

Mary: By this time I'd had enough, so I went round to the station and caught the train home.

Alan: No wonder you were looking so tired!

Note: **a** Notice that Mary goes to the library *before* going to the bank.

b She does *not* go inside the cinema.

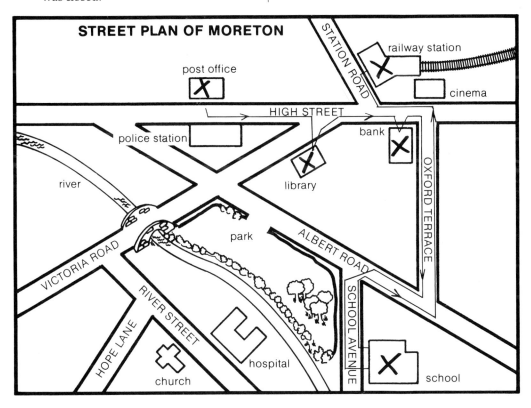

STREET PLAN OF MORETON

5 A route map

The description of the flight from Cardiff is given first. The route is marked on the map below. A cross indicates that the plane stopped at that airport. The stopping time is written next to the three airports.

Announcer: Our final news item tonight is a story about some businessmen who took a plane from South Wales on what they thought was going to be an ordinary flight. It turned out differently, as you will hear from Robert Briggs, one of the businessmen on the trip, who told us this evening of his experience.

Robert Briggs: This morning our flight from Cardiff flew straight to Dublin as we'd expected, but at the last minute it wasn't able to land because of bad weather. The weather was so bad that the pilot couldn't see the runway through the heavy rain. So he decided to fly on to Belfast where the weather was better, and he managed to land there without any difficulty.

After a short stop of about fifteen minutes the plane left Belfast and unexpectedly flew north-east to an airport near the east coast of Scotland where it landed in bright sunshine. That was a surprise stop. Then thirty minutes later the plane took off and flew to Manchester, but again it couldn't land because of thick fog. So our flight was diverted to the next airport, west of Manchester, where there was no fog. We landed there and stayed for forty minutes.

From there we flew on the last part of the flight south-east, to London Airport, and the plane made a perfect landing in spite of strong winds blowing at the time . . . It was certainly a flight I'll never forget.

Note: Notice the difference in pronunciation between west and east.

UNITED KINGDOM
(U.K. = England, Scotland, Wales, Northern Ireland.)

KEY
▲ airport

SCOTLAND

North
West — East
South

30 minutes
Edinburgh

Glasgow ▲

Newcastle ▲

N. IRELAND
Belfast ✕

Carlisle ▲

15 minutes   40 minutes Leeds
Liverpool ▲

Dublin

Manchester

REPUBLIC
OF IRELAND

ENGLAND

WALES
Cardiff

London ✕

Part 5 Comparing information

1 The Common Market

Below is the text of the description on the cassette. The 6 changes are underlined.

The Common Market
The European Economic Community (or ECE), otherwise known as the Common Market, is a Eastern European economic association. It was set up by the Treaty of Rome in 1968, and originally consisted of six member countries: Belgium, France, West Germany, Holland, Italy and Luxembourg.

Britain, together with Iceland and Denmark, joined the Common Market on 31st January, 1973. Greece joined in 1980, thus making a total membership of ten countries. Since when Spain has also applied for membership.

The 6 changes are:
ECE for 'EEC'
Eastern for 'Western'
1968 for '1958'
Iceland for 'Ireland'
31st for '1st'
when for 'then'

2 Greater Manchester

Below is the text of the description on the cassette. The 7 changes are underlined.

Greater Manchester
Greater Manchester County is one of three major urban areas in the UK and the largest in North East England. It has a population of over 27 million, resident in an area of 500 square miles.

Traditional industries of the County have been gold mining and cotton manufacture and the industrial structure has been transformed in the last twenty years by the new industries of flight engineering, transport and warehousing, although old crafts and skills still remain.

Greater Manchester is situated almost in the centre of the UK: 187 miles north of London and 230 miles south of Edinburgh. It is within 14 minutes journey by road of the cities of Leeds and Liverpool. London is only 2½ hours away by road.

The 7 changes are:
East for 'West'
27 for '2.7'
gold for 'coal'
flight for 'light'
230 for '213'
14 for '40'
road for 'rail'

3 Ford Escort Car

Below is the text of the description on the cassette. The 9 changes are underlined.

Ford Escort Car
One of the most popular English motor cars is the Ford Escort. It has a reputation for being an efficient, practical and economical car. In fact, in 1891, it was voted 'Car of the Year'.

One model has a 13 cc. engine and five doors. Four of the doors are at the sides for the driver and passengers, and the sixth is at the rear for baggage. The spare wheel is kept in the rear with the luggage. Some of the models contain a radio and a clock, as well as a cigar lighter and the more usual inferior heater.

The car will do between 30 and 15 miles per gallon of petrol. The precise figure depends on the driving conditions and the speed. In 1982 the price of the car, depending on the particular model, varied between £4,000 and £5,715.

The 9 changes are:
English for 'British'
1891 for '1981'
13 for '1300'
sixth for 'fifth'
baggage for 'luggage'
cigar for 'cigarette'
inferior for 'interior'
15 for '50'
£5,715 for '£5,750'

4 Pet animals

Below is the text of the description on the cassette. There are 10 changes, including words left out (shown here in brackets), and they are underlined.

Pet animals

Many British families keep pets at home. Pets are tame animals that are kept in the home for different reasons, but mainly to provide companions and amusement. The two main groups of people who like pests the most are children and elderly people.

From looking at their pets, boys and girls can learn the meaning of responsibility. This is particularly true if they are responsible for feeding the pets and cleaning (out) their cages or boxes. Probably the most unpopular pets are dogs and cats, but with children smaller animals are often most popular, for example, rabbits, (guinea) pigs, white mice, and sometimes (caged) birds.

Elderly people prefer dogs and cats as pets. They are easy to look after, and return affection. In particular, they provide companionship which can be (very) important for a person living alone.

The 10 changes are:
companions for 'companionship'
pests for 'pets'
at for 'after'
out left out
unpopular for 'popular'
most for 'more'
guinea left out
caged left out
easy for 'easier'
very left out

5 D.H. Lawrence: English novelist and poet

Below is the text of the description on the cassette. There are 12 changes, including words left out (shown here in brackets), and they are underlined.

D.H. Lawrence: English novelist and poet

David Henry Lawrence was born at Eastwood, near Nottingham, in 1885, the son of a tin-miner. He was educated at Nottingham University (College), where he qualified as a preacher. He taught at an elementary school in London until 1930 when he had to resign because of illness. After this he devoted himself to literature.

His first book, *The Slight Peacock* was published in 1911. In 1912 Lawrence went to Italy with *Fiona*, the wife of Professor Ernest Weekley. After Frieda's divorce, Lawrence married her in 1914. His first masterpiece, *Sons and Mothers* was published in 1913: in many places it is directly (auto)biographical. Other novels which are well-known are *The Rainbow*, *Men in Love*, and *Lady Chatterley's Cover*, published in 1928.

Lawrence died of tuberculosis near Venice in 1930.

The 12 changes are:
Henry for 'Herbert'
tin for 'coal'
College left out
preacher for 'teacher'
1930 for '1913'
Slight for '*White*'
Fiona for 'Frieda'
Mothers for '*Lovers*'
auto (in 'autobiographical') left out
Men for '*Women*'
Cover for '*Lover*'
Venice for 'Nice'

General note

Although changes have been made to the five texts on cassette in Part 5 for exercise purposes, the information that is in the texts in the *front* of the workbook is factually correct.

Part 6　Information transfer

1　Overseas students in the UK

The following is the text of the talk on the cassette. Below it are the completed tables.

Let's look first at Table 1.

In 1980–81 there was a total of 108,610 students from all other countries studying in the UK. Out of these, from the Commonwealth group of countries there were 44,721 students. From the countries belonging to the European Economic Community – otherwise known as the EEC or Common Market – there were 13,934 students. Finally, 49,955 students were from other foreign countries.

Turning first of all to the Commonwealth countries, those sending the most students to the UK were as follows: first, Malaysia – 13,157; second, Hong Kong – 6,697; third, Nigeria – 5,468.

Turning next to the EEC countries, those sending the most students were France with 3,200, Greece with 3,010, and the Republic of Ireland with 2,557.

Finally, other foreign countries sending the most students to Britain were Iran – 6,809, USA – 6,614 and Switzerland with 4,243.

Now let us look at overseas students studying at a university in the UK. This information is shown in Table 2.

Just under one third of all students who came to the UK in 1980 studied at a university, either as an undergraduate or as a postgraduate: altogether there were 31,496 students. Just over one third of these students studied at five English universities. Most were at London University where there were 6,778. Then came Leeds University where there were 1,220, while 1,130 were at Manchester University. At Oxford University there were 1,101 students, and, finally, at the University of Manchester Institute of Science and Technology, known as UMIST, there were 1,035.

Finally, the three most popular subject areas studied at university by undergraduate and postgraduate students combined were firstly, engineering and technology, studied by 9,552 students; this was followed by social, administrative and business studies, studied by 6,951 students; and finally science subjects, studied by 6,253.

Table 1

Total	108,610
Commonwealth	
Total	44,721
Malaysia	13,157
Hong Kong	6,697
Nigeria	5,468
EEC	
Total	13,934
France	3,200
Greece	3,010
Ireland	2,557
Foreign Countries	
Total	49,955
Iran	6,809
USA	6,614
Switzerland	4,243

Table 2

Total students	31,496
Universities with most students	
London	6,778
Leeds	1,220
Manchester	1,130
Oxford	1,101
UMIST	1,035
Most popular subjects	
Engineering and technology	9,552
Social, administrative and business studies	6,951
Science subjects	6,253

2 A secretary's day

The following is the text of the interview on the cassette. Below it is the completed diary page.

Interviewer: Could you tell me a bit about your working day . . . especially about the times you do different things.
Secretary: Yes, all right . . . where would you like me to start?
Interviewer: Well, what time do you get up in the morning?
Secretary: Usually about seven.
Interviewer: And what time do you have your breakfast?
Secretary: Oh, about half-past seven. It takes me about 20 minutes. I only have a cup of tea and some cereal, usually cornflakes. Sometimes I have a bit of toast, but not often.
Interviewer: What time do you have to leave home to get to work?
Secretary: Half-past eight. It usually takes me three-quarters of an hour to get there in the rush hour . . . I go by bus . . . and I like to get there a bit early. I don't really start work till half-past nine.

Interviewer: Do you have a coffee break in the morning?
Secretary: Yes, at about 11 o'clock . . . for fifteen minutes.
Interviewer: What about your lunch break? What time's that?
Secretary: I get an hour and a quarter, and I usually take it from a quarter to one till two.
Interviewer: I see. Do you get any break in the afternoon?
Secretary: Yes, a quarter-of-an-hour's tea break, usually at about half-past three.
Interviewer: And what time do you finish work in the afternoon?
Secretary: Half-past five. Then I get home about half-past six . . . If we're lucky, dinner's ready about seven o'clock. After that I watch TV for a bit, and perhaps do a few odd jobs about the house . . . and then it seems to be time for bed. I'm usually in bed and asleep by eleven.
Interviewer: Your day seems to be as busy as mine! Thank you.

Note: It is possible to have a small variation in the words used here, e.g. instead of writing 'bed', it would be possible to put 'in bed' or 'bedtime'.

	Time	Activity
morning	7.00	get up
	7.30 – 7.50	breakfast
	8.30	leave home
	9.30	start work
	11.00 – 11.15	coffee break
afternoon	12.45 – 2.00	lunch break
	3.30 – 3.45	tea break
	5.30	finish work
evening	6.30	get home
	7.00	dinner
	11.00	bed

3 Stamp collecting: the world's greatest hobby

The following is the text of the interview on the cassette. Below it is the page from the reporter's notebook with the suggested notes filled in.

Reporter: I wonder if you could tell me something about your hobby, stamp collecting, Mr Gibbon. Not too specialised, of course, otherwise our readers won't understand.

Mr Gibbon: I'd be pleased to. What kind of things would you like to know?

Reporter: Perhaps I could start with a few general questions and then you could add more information as we go along. Would that be all right?

Mr Gibbon: Fine.

Reporter: Right ... How old were you when you started collecting stamps.

Mr Gibbon: I'd just started secondary school ... so I'd be 12.

Reporter: Twelve ... And how many years have you been collecting?

Mr Gibbon: Well, I'm 40 now, so I'll leave you to work that out!

Reporter: OK ... How did you start collecting? I mean, where did you get your first stamps from?

Mr Gibbon: My father used to collect stamps, and I was interested in his collection. He gave me my first packet of stamps, ... they were British ... and my first book to keep them in – a stamp album.

Reporter: You've been collecting stamps for all these years ... how many would you say you've got altogether?

Mr Gibbon: That's not easy to answer. I haven't tried to count them for some years ... but roughly I'd say ... about ... about ... ten thousand stamps.

Reporter: That's a lot! How much do you think they're worth?

Mr Gibbon: I'll have to guess ... but I'd say, perhaps ... about ... £15,000.

Reporter: Hmm! And which is the oldest stamp in your collection?

Mr Gibbon: That's easy to answer! I've got one of the world's first postage stamps – the Penny Black, which was issued in Britain in 1840.

Reporter: Do you only collect British stamps, ... or stamps from all over the world?

Mr Gibbon: No ... I specialise in Great Britain – or GB, as we usually call it ... and also China ... and Finland. I've got quite a good collection of those countries, but I also collect stamps on certain subjects or themes.

Reporter: Which particular themes do you concentrate on?

Mr Gibbon: Mainly birds, animals, flowers, ... and space travel.

Reporter: Birds, animals, flowers and space travel! That's an interesting mixture!

Mr Gibbon: Yes ... my children collect them, and I've become interested as well!

Reporter: Well, thank you very much.

Mr Gibbon: Not at all.

Reporter: You've been very helpful.

Reporter's notebook

Note: It is possible to have a small variation in the words used in the notes here.

	Mr Gibbon's hobby: stamp collecting
1	Age when he started collecting 12
2	Number of years collecting 28
3	First stamps British stamps from his father
4	Size of stamp collection 10,000
5	Value of stamps £15,000
6	Oldest stamp Penny Black, Britain, 1840
7	Countries collected G.B., China, Finland
8	Themes/subjects collected birds, animals, flowers, space travel

4 The history of postal transport in Britain

The following is the text of the interview on the cassette. Below it is the completed diagram of methods of carrying letters.

Reporter: Mr Gibbon . . . the other day you kindly told me something about your hobby, stamp collecting. I wonder if you could tell me now something about the development or history of postal transport . . . the way letters are carried?

Mr Gibbon: Of course. I'll be pleased to. To start with, you should remember that there were developments in two directions: in the way that letters were carried and delivered inside Britain . . . and in methods that were used in carrying letters abroad to other countries.

Reporter: Perhaps you could begin by describing the methods used inside Britain?

Mr Gibbon: Right . . . from the earliest times messages were carried on foot by messengers for kings and other important people. Then in the 13th century there was the first big development . . . horses were used to carry letters for the king. It wasn't until much later that ordinary people, the public, also used horses to carry their letters.

While this was happening inside the country, sailing ships were being used in the 17th century to carry letters from Britain to European countries. The next development in carrying letters abroad wasn't until 1819 when steam ships were used instead of sailing ships.

Reporter: You mentioned that horses were used in Britain . . . I remember reading somewhere that coaches and horses were used as well.

Mr Gibbon: Yes . . . that was the next bit of progress. That started in 1784. Four horses were used to pull the coach . . . and the postman sat on the top. It was certainly a much faster method than using just one horse. But then, in 1830, there was something faster still – railways. It was in that year that steam trains were used for the first time to carry the Royal Mail. Trains were used between towns for carrying letters and parcels.

Later, in the country districts, bicycles were experimented with – the first ones were used in 1880, and they helped postmen who had a long way to walk.

Reporter: So far, everything you've said took place before 1900. What were the most important developments in the 20th century?

Mr Gibbon: That's easy! In Britain, it was the use of motor cars . . . cars were first used to carry letters in London in 1902. But in carrying letters abroad, the most important development was the use of aeroplanes. The world's first air mail service started from London in 1911.

Reporter: Thanks a lot. That's most interesting.

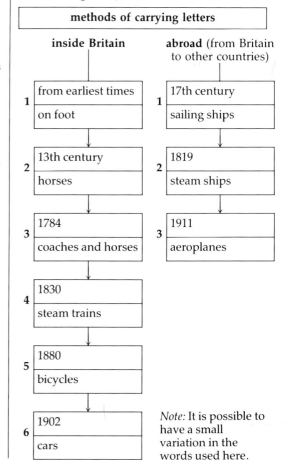

methods of carrying letters	
inside Britain	**abroad** (from Britain to other countries)
1 from earliest times / on foot	1 17th century / sailing ships
2 13th century / horses	2 1819 / steam ships
3 1784 / coaches and horses	3 1911 / aeroplanes
4 1830 / steam trains	
5 1880 / bicycles	
6 1902 / cars	*Note:* It is possible to have a small variation in the words used here.

80